ZEN SPEAKS

SHOUTS OF NOTHINGNESS

Adapted and Illustrated by Tsai Chih Chung
Translated by Brian Bruya

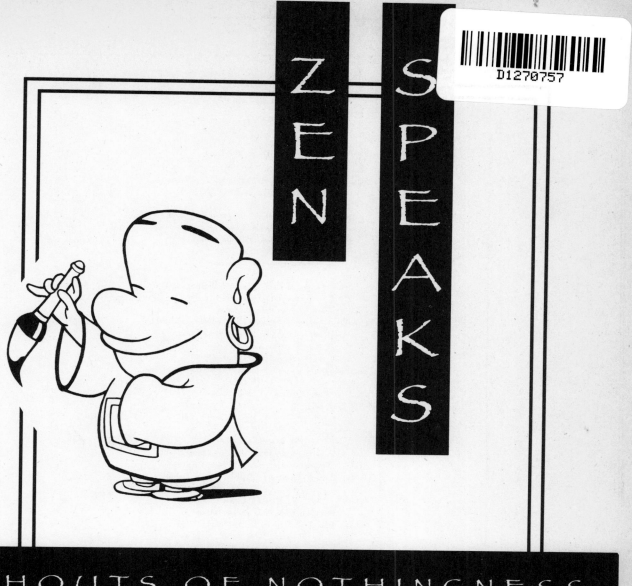

ANCHOR BOOKS
DOUBLEDAY
NEW YORK LONDON TORONTO SYDNEY AUCKLAND

An Anchor Book
PUBLISHED BY DOUBLEDAY
a division of Bantam Doubleday Dell Publishing Group, Inc.
1540 Broadway, New York, NY 10036

Calligraphy by Brent Carpenter

Library of Congress Cataloging-in-Publication Data
Ts'ai, Chih-chung, 1948-
[Ch'an shuo. English]
Zen speaks : shouts of nothingness / adapted and illustrated by
Tsai Chih Chung ; translated by Brian Bruya.
p. cm.
Translation of: Ch'an shuo.
1. Zen Buddhism—Caricatures and cartoons. I. Bruya, Brian,
1966- . II. Title.
BQ9265.6.T7313 1994
294.3'927—dc20 93-5405
CIP

ISBN 0-385-47257-9

Printed in the United States of America
First Anchor Books Edition: May 1994
10 9 8 7 6 5 4 3 2 1

Contents

Translator's Preface

When the first book in this series, *Zhuangzi Speaks*, came out in America, a common initial response was, "It's very charming, but what is it?" I see now that this is understandable since these books are comic books first of all, and comic books about Chinese philosophy and literature on top of that. For those who would like to know more about how the book came to be, I offer the following short introduction.

Tsai Chih Chung (C. C. Tsai) is the most accomplished and popular cartoonist in all of East Asia, and several of his books have been incorporated into the public school curriculum in Japan. C. C. Tsai began his career at the age of sixteen by publishing the first of what would be approximately two hundred "action" comic books. Following that, he went into the field of animation and garnered himself the Chinese equivalent of our Oscar, while building up the largest animation company in Taiwan. In his spare time, he turned to the humor of comic strips and put out the first daily comic strip in Taiwan newspapers.

One day on a flight to Japan, he began to sketch scenes from a book he was reading. The book had been written over two thousand years ago by a famous Daoist (Taoist) thinker named Zhuangzi (Chuang Tsu). From this emerged a new genre in the book world—a serious (though lighthearted) comic book explicating a profound topic. His aim was not to simplify, but to clarify. The ancient language in China is difficult for modern people to understand, so in addition to illustrating the subject matter, he also wrote the text in Modern Chinese.

When *Zhuangzi Speaks* came out in Taiwan, it shot to the top of the bestseller list, and the head of a major publishing company immediately remarked that it had world potential. Tired of animation by now, C. C. sold off his company and spent all of his efforts on the daily strips and his new series on ancient Chinese thought, both of which were bringing him unparalleled fame for a cartoonist. Soon he held the four highest spots atop the bestseller list, until other authors insisted that comic books no longer be included on the list of serious literature. There are now over twenty books in C. C.'s series and millions of copies in print, and his books are rapidly gaining popularity all over the world.

Zen Speaks, as the title suggests, is about Zen Buddhism, which is more of an attitude toward life than a system of strict religious beliefs. The episodes depicted are for the most part short dialogues between various well-known Zen masters and their students. Most are drawn directly from pre-modern Zen source literature, from such books as the *Platform Sutra of the Sixth Patriarch*, the *Transmission of the Lamp*, the *Gateless Gate (Mumonkan)*, the *Blue Cliff Record*, and the *Record of Linji (Rinzai)*. C. C. translated the laconic Classical Chinese into highly readable yet technically accurate Modern Chinese, which I have done my best to render into familiar, idiomatic English, taking care not to oversimplify.

Because the history of Zen Buddhism spans a

period of over two millennia and was expounded by numerous Zen masters speaking various languages, the names of all these people can become rather confusing. To keep you from tripping over all the names, I have attempted to simplify and clarify in the following ways:

1) You will find a quick and easy-to-follow pronunciation guide for Chinese names in the back. I encourage you to use it, as the pronunciation of a Chinese name spelled in English is not necessarily self-evident.

2) Names of Indians are spelled from the Sanskrit; names of Chinese are spelled from the Chinese; and names of Japanese are spelled from the Japanese. This may seem the obvious thing to do, but it is not always the case. It may also be worth noting here that I do not follow this pattern for other technical terms; instead, I use the Japanese *Zen* rather than the Chinese *Chan* or Sanskrit *Dhyāna*; I use "emptiness" rather than the Sanskrit *sūnyatā*; and I use the original Sanskrit *Nirvāna*, rather than, say, "bliss" or "extinction."

3) An unfortunate circumstance in regard to Chinese translation is that one system of Romanization gained almost universal acceptance for a time, then China switched to another system, and the rest of the world has been trying to catch up ever since. I use this relatively new system, called *pinyin*, and for well-known names I include the old system in parentheses.

In regard to the Chinese at the margin of each page, it is retained nominally for reference purposes, as it contains the original text in some places and notes thrown in by the original Chinese editor in other places. More to the point, it is a nice decorative touch; the reader shouldn't get the impression that he or she is missing out on any essential information.

I should also add a note here on the *sauvastika* 卍 that appears on illustrations of the Buddha and on some monasteries. It is an auspicious diagram from ancient India that has come to be a symbol of Buddhism in China. It should be distinguished from the *svastika* 卐 and its associations of horror from recent Western history.

Many thanks are due to Professor Robert Buswell of UCLA for vetting my translation and suggesting useful corrections. Any errors that remain are my own.

—B. B.

Introduction

According to the ninth-century Chan (Zen) master Liangjie of Dongshan (807–869, see p. 136 of *Zen Speaks*) the people of his time were encumbered by too much idle knowledge. This he attributed to three forms of defilement. "The first is defiled views. This is not departing from a particular fixed view about the nature of Awakening and thus falling into a sea of poison. The second is defiled emotions. This is entrapment in preferences and repulsions, thus having one's perspective become one-sided and rigid. The third is defiled language. This is mastering trivia and losing sight of the essential. The potential for Awakening is thoroughly obscured."[1] Ignorance, of which idle knowledge is one aspect, is held by Buddhists to be the root cause of suffering.

Most ninth-century Chinese Buddhists saw their time as one of great suffering, a Dharma-ending age. Though there have been people in every period of history who expressed a similar pessimism about the state of society and who saw fixed opinions and emotional attachments as contributing factors, Liangjie's identification of defiled language as one of the principle agents in his society's malaise is somewhat unique and resonates ominously with affairs in our own time. Language, the system by which a society produces and transmits its knowledge, is the preoccupation in the modern world of our news and entertainment industries as well as of our institutions and learning and research. The power of these industries and institutions to use or manipulate language, and hence knowledge, has been revolutionized by the invention of a new language, the language of the computer. An exponential explosion of information/knowledge has resulted, the effects of which are being felt far more pervasively than for any previous system of knowledge. Accompanying this knowledge explosion, and perhaps partly on account of it, has come increased specialization, the mastery of one small body of knowledge or technology. Even up to a few decades ago it was optimistically asserted that this growing mass of knowledge would lead to a gradual but inevitable improvement in the quality of life and would greatly reduce if not eliminate the bulk of human suffering. Now, many are not so sure. Much, if not most, of the knowledge proffered on television and in the classroom is, in fact, quite trivial in the sense that it generally has minimal bearing on an individual's everyday affairs or the deep-seated problems that confront modern society. All of this has led to questions about the nature and function of our knowledge-producing institutions and their product. To what end and for whose benefit is knowledge sought? To put the question in terms a Buddhist might use, how does a society's knowledge alleviate suffering either of the individual or all life?

It is to just such questions as these concerning the nature of knowledge and who controls it that a small but vigorous group of medieval East Asian Buddhists were responding in a most unique fashion. They, too, lived in a society in which the amount of knowledge had exploded due to a major influx of Buddhist texts and teachers from India and Central Asia. It was widely held that the knowledge contained in those texts and in the minds of their teachers was of vital importance to the welfare of the individual, the family, and the society as a whole. This knowledge came packaged in South and Central Asian languages utterly incomprehensible to most Chinese. Hence, the ability to use and manipulate these languages was a skill that conferred elite status and authority on the few so talented. In addition, the texts were so varied and diverse that people came to specialize in one kind of Buddhist knowledge or another. This powerful and influential medieval knowledge industry came increasingly under critical scrutiny from a group known as Chan Buddhists. It is this group of Buddhists that Tsai Chih Chung has brought to cartoon life in *Zen Speaks*.

Chan/Zen Buddhism

The word "Chan" is an abbreviation of "*channa*," a Chinese translation of the Indian Sanskrit term "*dhyāna*," or "meditation." In Japanese, the Chinese character for "*chan*," is read "*zen*," the term by which this form of Buddhism is most commonly known in Europe and America today. One of the characteristics of Chinese civilization was its tendency to bureaucratize almost every aspect of social and religious life. Chinese Buddhist monasteries were no exception; monks were organized into groups with clearly defined duties and privileges. Certain groups of monks were designated preachers, others reciters, others disciplinarians, and still others mediators. Chan monks appear to have had some connection with the group whose primary occupation within the monastic institution was to meditate. Most of what we know about the Chan monks is contained in a distinctive genre of Buddhist literature, known variously as "lamp records" or "discourse records." These texts were first compiled and published in China around the tenth century and their production has continued up to the modern period throughout China, Korea, and Japan.

Chan came to public attention in China as a distinct form of Buddhism sometime around the end of the seventh century. There appeared a group of monks at that time acting and talking in ways that challenged the kinds of knowledge and technologies that Chinese Buddhists and the society at large had held in highest esteem for generations. Their religious practices and modes of discourse bore little resemblance to those of either their predecessors or fellow Buddhists. Not only did they not do what was expected, they often engaged in actions that would have been regarded by Buddhist and non-Buddhist alike as quite shocking. Almost nowhere in this literature do we read that they studied, recited, or expounded the Buddhist scriptures, known as sutras. Yet those very scriptures were regarded by almost all Buddhists as nothing less than the words and fundamental insights of the Buddha himself. Study of these texts was fundamental to monastic training. Worse, these audacious monks often seemed to treat the scriptures with downright disrespect. In addition, they are almost never represented as engaging in meditation, in spite of the central role that practice has played in most Buddhist traditions. And contrary to most Chinese pedagogic practice, those regarded as masters or teachers generally responded to queries from apparently earnest seekers in what seems a most illogical, dismissive, or even abusive manner.

To appreciate who they were and what the significance of their behavior and thought was, it is useful to understand something of the medieval world of which they were a part, the political, social, and religious institutions that called forth their unconventional behavior.

The Medieval Chinese Knowledge Establishment

Chan arose in China during a period in which Buddhism was enjoying immense popular support ranging all the way from lowly peasants to the nobility and often reaching even to the emperor himself. Though it had its critics, Buddhism was championed by some of the most educated and elite members of Tang (618–907) Chinese society. In Changan, the Tang capital, the number and size of Buddhist temples and monasteries generally far surpassed those of the Taoist temples. These massive complexes were constructed by China's most skilled craftsmen from the finest woods and filled with beautifully carved or cast images of the buddhas and bodhisattvas. One catches glimpses of some of these images, discreetly placed in the background of a number of Tsai Chih Chung's drawings. Elaborate and detailed paintings of Buddhist paradises covered the walls. Hand-copied Buddhist scriptures and commentaries, numbering in the hundreds and, in some temples, thousands of volumes, filled their libraries. The sounds of chanting and of the great temple bells and drums were omnipresent around these establishments. The smell of incense imported from Central Asia filled the air. These medieval Buddhist monastic complexes were truly centers of wealth, knowledge, and power, resembling, if not matching, that of the imperial palace itself. This is not surprising since much of the wealth that went into the monasteries had come from the imperial coffers and donations from the nobility of Changan. Chan monks appear to have been peripheral to much of this power and wealth in the beginning.

It might be assumed that religious knowledge, such as that set forth by Buddhists, though perhaps philosophically demanding at times, was otherwise a relatively simple matter, particularly when compared to the complexity of modern knowledge. But in the eyes of the medieval Chinese who for hundreds of years were the recipients of what must have seemed an endless stream of Buddhist texts and teachings flowing out of India, it, no doubt, appeared utterly overwhelming. This knowledge dealt with a wide range of topics from a variety of standpoints that were often in conflict with each other. The problem was threefold. First, the texts had to be translated from Serindic languages radically different in structure and style from Chinese. Second, once translated, the great number and variety of Buddhist scriptures made available in Chinese could be read only by the literate few, an exceedingly small minority. Third, study of the scriptures revealed unexpected contradictions and ambiguities in the teachings. China's Confucian traditions had long elevated the role of the scholar as interpreter of difficult and arcane knowledge. Thus, the obvious solution to this threefold problem was to create and fund research complexes within certain of the elite monasteries in which highly trained scholar-monks could translate, study, and interpret these scriptures. Many of the monks who devoted much of their lives to work within these institutes rose to the highest status within the Chinese Buddhist establishment. Their output was prodigious and highly regarded in elite society.

These research complexes, rather than attempting to account for the entire corpus of Buddhist teachings, tended to specialize in one or a group of related scriptures with a particular orientation distinct from those of other scriptures. Thus monks became specialists in interpreting certain types of Buddhist teachings. It was also their responsibility to provide oral commentary on their scriptural specialties for the benefit of the general public, and particularly the illiterate. Implicit in their approach was the well-respected notion that a long and arduous course of scripture study would eventuate in an authoritative knowledge, if not the supreme goal, of Awakening. These monks were one of the dominant factions in the monasteries of Changan.

Another powerful faction among the monks of Changan were specialists in particular technologies for acquiring Buddhist wisdom less dependent on texts. These technologies included programmed visualization practices by which mediators could project themselves into resplendent otherworldly realms, "Pure Lands," and come face-to-face with spiritual teachers and bodhisattvas (saviors). The models for these realms generally came directly from the scriptures. Other monks specialized in the ritual technologies to be used on special occasions, such as funerals. Pilgrimage to distant sacred Buddhist sites and relic worship were also popular practices in medieval China.

Outside the Buddhist establishment, a small but influential body of Taoists taught technologies by which the practitioner could bring him or herself into a vibrant state of physical health and well-being, a state regarded as necessary, though not sufficient, for acquiring the knowledge of self-transformation techniques leading to transcendence. These technologies for cultivating one's life energies included highly controlled dietary and exercise regimes, visualizations, the study of texts, and minutely articulated sexual practices. The heirs of this now fractured tradition can be seen among the Taiji Quan and Qigong practitioners in most parks throughout China today. With some imagination they might also be seen in the aerobics studios and pure food cafés of our own time. Thus, the Tang knowledge establishment was a world of scholars, rhetoricians, visualization and ritual specialists, and body workers.

Radical Buddhism

Huineng, also known as the Sixth Patriarch (638–713, see p. 120), has become in the lore of Chan Buddhism over the last thousand years perhaps its most popular and representative figure. He is conspicuously represented as an illiterate from South China, a country boy. His appearance and demeanor were so uncouth, in fact, that his master directed him away from the halls of scripture study and meditation to work as an ordinary laborer at the grinding wheel in the monastery granary. When it came time to pass the mantle of succession, in this case a robe and bowl, Huineng's master invited all the monks in the monastery to demonstrate their wisdom in whatever way they chose so as to determine the individual most worthy. The clear favorite was the monastery's head monk, Shenxiu, a literate and highly cultivated man. He demonstrated his wisdom by means of a poem, that he wrote on the wall of a temple corridor.

> The body is the tree of Awakening
> The mind is like a clear mirror.
> At all times we must strive to polish it,
> And must not let the dust collect.[2]

The poem is a distilled portrait of the Buddhist monastic impulse. The role of the monk was to strive through various practices, but particularly meditation, to free his mind from the defilements that distorted his view of reality. Ignorance thus dispelled, Awakening would ensue.

The other monks were duly impressed and, certain that the head monk would be designated the master's successor, immediately committed the poem to memory so that they could continue to recite it as they went about their monastic duties. Overhearing this poem, Huineng composed a poetic response that he had a literate monk record for him on the same corridor wall.

> Awakening originally has no tree,
> The mirror also has no stand.
> Buddha nature is always clean and pure,
> Where is there room for dust?[3]

Huineng's verse called into question the most basic of monastic practices including meditation, or, more to the point, their motivation, the purification of the mind. This so impressed his master that he passed the robe and bowl to Huineng, though in an atmosphere of great secrecy.

This legend sounds most of the themes that come to characterize Chan Buddhism in its assault on the Tang establishment. Many of these same themes are echoed in *Zen Speaks*, Huineng's illiteracy and his apparent lack of exposure to scripture or commentaries stands out in stark contrast to the rich literary-scholarly training of Shenxiu. Not only is Huineng illiterate, but his duties as a common laborer place him at the periphery of the monastic institution, and for that matter of respectable status in Chinese society at large. He hardly functions as a monk at all, since he appears not to study scriptures or meditate. Nor does he memorize and recite the scriptures. No idle knowledge here, just everyday chores. But when called upon, his undefiled mind shone forth with overwhelming brilliance. Not only did Huineng's poem call monastic practices into question, implicit in its focus on mind was the Chan disdain of body cultivation practices. More important than what he said, the kind of person he was characterized as being called into question the grand monastic establishment of Tang China with its scholar—monks and monopolistic claim on knowledge.

That the legend was rhetorical, and not to be taken as a model for behavior, is clear from what we know of Chan monks, including the compilers of the legend. Most were, in fact, quite literate. They demonstrated an informed knowledge of most of the important Buddhist scriptures, and they practiced meditation. To be unaware of this fact is to risk missing the point of the legend, not to mention the anecdotes in this book. One of its earliest functions was to cast doubt on the knowledge claims of the Changan Buddhist elite, and hence on their authority and power. It was, in fact, a play for power, pure and simple. Be that as it may, the legend established a set of themes that became fundamental to the way Chan developed and understood itself in later Chinese history. All of these themes are rooted in a particular understanding of wisdom as something opposed to mere knowledge.

Embodied Scripture

A common theme in this literature is the misdirection of most scholarly effort in its excessive specialization and verbose explications. Such effort was regarded as misdirected for at least two reasons. On a theoretical level, it failed to take seriously some of its fundamental doctrines. On a practical level, it was pedagogically counterproductive. The doctrine of *Emptiness*, referred to several times in *Zen Speaks*, was one of the principal teachings carried by Buddhist monks into China. Ironically, it was one of the most difficult to understand, growing as it did out of complex philosophical debates that took place in India four hundred years after the Buddha's death. Though its philosophical complexities were probably understood by only a minority of people in the Tang period, it had an immense influence on the development of Chinese Buddhist thought and practice.

Without going into the philosophical intricacies of the Emptiness doctrine, we can simply note here that it led to a form of radical non-dualism. The implications of this view were that, in theory, distinctions between wisdom and ignorance, the mundane and transcendental realms, sacred and profane, mind and matter, were dualistic and, hence, unjustified. This non-dualism coincided with another teaching entering China at the same time, namely that all beings were born with buddha-nature, a doctrine maintaining that wisdom is innate in all beings. The question follows that if one has buddha-nature and if ignorance is not different from wisdom, why isn't everyone wise and buddhas? A simplified answer would be that we all are wise, but that we simply aren't yet awake (Sanskrit: *bud*, from which comes Buddha, the "Awakened One"). Thus one shouldn't need to be told what Emptiness or the Truth is, since we are already all in full possession of that. What is necessary is to wake up. However, in practice, many of the same teachers who lectured on

Emptiness engaged in and encouraged the study of scriptures in order to gain wisdom. They taught techniques for escaping this world and being reborn in "Pure Land." They engaged in meditation in order to escape from impure, defiled states of mind into a pure, blissful state. Hence, implicit in their practices was a dualistic understanding. It was clearly the case that for most the view of Emptiness remained just that, a view that conflicted with their dualistic approach to practice. In reaction to this, the Chan monks attempted to align their practices with their understanding of the Buddhist notion of Emptiness. How they did that is what *Zen Speaks* is about.

There arises the problem of how to teach that which needn't, indeed, can't be taught. To emphasize the study of scripture leads to a focus on an external object as a source of wisdom, at the expense of the subject, the individual's own mind. If one were to awake, it could only come through sensitivity to one's own mind; excessive focus on texts or techniques, it was felt, would only serve to deaden that sensitivity. That one might have, instead of an "excessive focus," an informed awareness of the scriptures and not thereby become insensitive to one's mind appears consistent with the behavior of the authors of this literature. Hence, their critique is directed not so much at the scriptures themselves, but rather at the disembodied and counterproductive exposition of them. The wisdom that is the object of the Buddhist scriptures, if not embodied, is no wisdom at all, simply idle knowledge. This principle can be found underlying most Chan anecdotes. The principle is made explicit in the anecdote in which the disciple burns the precious book given him by his master, a teacher of "Zen not reliant on the written word." (see p. 50.) The master is brought to task for not embodying his own teaching. The famous thirteenth-century Japanese Zen monk Dogen wrote, "To understand these scriptures is to make of them . . . one's own body and mind . . . it is to make of them one's own bed and walking. . . . the behavior of a master, like his washing his face or his drinking tea, is not different from the teaching to be found in scriptures; in fact, it is an old scripture itself."[4] It will be noted in these anecdotes that the context in which teaching is sought, transmitted, or realized is rarely a traditional one, such as a lecture hall where the scriptures would be expounded. Rather the context is most commonly the scene of some ordinary activity, such as a bathtub (see p. 54), the vegetable drying yard (see p. 60), the outlots of a temple (see p. 107), or in the grinding room as in the case of Huineng.

Embodied Teaching

The teacher in this tradition, rather than being uncooperative as he sometimes appears to be, is actually quite compassionate. To provide a student with simple or straightforward explanations in a conventional manner, no matter how valid, would only reinforce the student's counterproductive habit of looking for wisdom outside of him or herself. Thus, the ideal teacher would not only seek to embody or manifest "buddha-mind" openly in his own behavior for the sake of the student, but he would seek to jar the student back into his or her own mind. The role of the teacher, then, is not to give the student knowledge, but to put them on track in the only place they can discover wisdom, that is, in their own minds. What is important in these anecdotes is, first and foremost, not the content of what a master says, but *how* what he says forces the student back into his or her own mind. The angry response brought forth by Yizhong's splashing ink on a monk's forehead (see p. 61) revealed that monk's mind—in action. This is known in Chan literature as "direct pointing." Just as striking a student, grabbing him by the nose, or shouting at him induces an immediate and visceral response, words used in a demonstrative way can potentially do the same thing. Words used to convey information rarely call forth any such response.

The alert reader may ask at this point why Tsai's chubby little monk interpreter in *Zen Speaks* appears at the end of each anecdote to inform us in a simple and direct fashion what message we should take from the incident. Wouldn't this be defeating the purpose of these anecdotes by turning performance into information? On one level the answer is yes. Simply as a point of history, however, our monk-interpreter is doing exactly what Chan teachers have done for generations, and in fact still do today, comment or give lectures on Chan anecdotes. Practically speaking, this is not so misguided. Just as most modern world citizens, whether in China, Japan, or America, are unfamiliar with the bulk of Buddhist scriptures or teachings, so most Chinese over the past thousand years, whether because of illiteracy or lack of exposure, were unfamiliar with much of the doctrine underlying these stories. The success of these anecdotes depends on intimate familiarity with knowledge of scripture left unstated, but that is nonetheless common knowledge. As in many jokes, the laugh or jolt comes when the punch line collides with that unstated but accepted knowledge. On the other hand, monks by virtue of their monastic training would normally have been familiar with the issues raised in the anecdotes, in fact may have thought of raising those issue themselves, and hence would have less need for such informational aids.

Whereas most monks wouldn't have needed the informational aids provided in commentaries, the fact that many read these anecdotes with the intention of shortcutting the process of grappling with them, is repeatedly confirmed in the literature. Their misguided strategy was to memorize the demonstrative responses made by successful predecessors, and to mimic or "parrot" those responses as a means of demonstrating their own embodiment of the teaching. That these strategies were doomed to failure seems obvious, yet much of what passes as individualism today is nothing more. One might go equally wrong in focusing only on the meaning of the anecdotes here.

This Land Is the Pure Land

Just as these anecdotes represent the Chan master engaged in practices and dialogues in such a way as not to make distinctions between teaching and teacher, so they also represent the material world and nature as not different from mind. Distinctions between mind and matter are no less dualistic than those between ignorance and wisdom. When Weiyan let out a hearty laugh on seeing the clouds part in the mountains, he manifested this awareness (see p. 74). And when the seeker visits a Zen master (see p. 45), he is asked if he had "heard the sound of the hollow" through which he passed on his way. We mistake the point of these anecdotes if we see them as simply encouraging nature appreciation. The seeker is being told in a non-pedantic manner not to make dualistic distinctions between the mind of the Zen master and the natural world.

Liangjie of Dongshan, whose disparaging comments on the idle knowledge of his day opened these remarks, once asked his master about the Chan notion that non-sentient beings (matter) could, like Buddhist masters, teach the Way. At one point in the exchange he is referred to the following line in the *Amitābha Sutra*, a popular Buddhist scripture, "Water birds, tree groves, all without exception recite the Buddha's name, recite the Truth (Dharma)."[5] This line in the sutra is spoken by the Buddha as he is describing the Pure Land, a realm into which many hoped to be reborn as a result of certain prescribed acts performed in this world. The use of this line by Liangjie's master is significant here for two reasons. First it is intended as a description of natural phenomenon in this world, not of a transcendent paradise, and second, it suggests poetically that natural phenomena, not just enlightened masters, "expound" ultimate truths. In both of these radically non-dualistic perspectives Chan was challenging the knowledge establishment of its day. If the Pure Land is wherever one is, there is no need for the expensive or time-consuming technologies for getting there. It is only necessary to understand where one is. Moreover, if it is understood that nature teaches, then scholarly institutes cease to be the sole arbitrators of knowledge.

These then are some of the ways that medieval Chan masters challenged the Tang knowledge establishment and its great mass of "idle knowledge." Rather than providing explanations of such Buddhist doctrines as Emptiness, as scholars and conventional teachers were doing, they sought to embody the doctrine in their behavior and speech. Rather than presenting arguments on behalf of or opposing certain theories of Emptiness, as rhetoricians were doing, they engaged in a demonstrative form of rhetoric, that, though it revealed a profound grasp of the scriptures, did not make use of specialized knowledge and erudition to make its points. By directing seekers back into their own minds as the seat of Awakening and away from sages, saviors, or distant Pure Lands, they juxtaposed themselves to those who offered special techniques for obtaining widsom. Finally, by insisting that wisdom was inseparable from embodiment, they placed themselves in opposition to those who sought to first transform the body as a means to achieve wisdom. As important as what they were seeking to achieve was, how they went about achieving it is of greater importance. As in some martial arts theories, one seeks to avoid joining battle with an opponent head-on or on his or her own ground. So these Chan anecdotes replace argument and exegesis with "direct pointing" and embodiment. It was a form of intellectual judo, offering no clear target to its opponents. Not only was this approach not openly aggressive, it was executed with a sense of humor that is part of its appeal. But though there is much humor in this literature, that fact should not lead us to regard it lightly. It is, on the whole, profoundly serious.

William Powell is a professor of Chinese religions at the University of California at Santa Barbara and is the translator of *The Record of Tung-shan*.

Notes:

1. *The Record of Tung-shan*, translated by William Powell (Honolulu: Univ. of Hawaii Press, 1989), p. 66.
2. Adapted from Philip Yampolsky's translation of the *Platform Sutra of the Sixth Patriarch* (New York: Columbia University Press, 1967), p. 130.
3. Adapted from Yampolsky, p. 132.
4. Dogen, *Shobogenzo*, translated by Allan Grapard.
5. *The Record of Tung-shan*, p. 26.

ZEN IS:

Not reliant on the written word,

A special transmission
separate from the scriptures;

Direct pointing at one's mind,

Seeing one's nature,
becoming a Buddha.

—Bodhidharma
(?–528 A.D.)

達摩大師說：「不立文字，教外別傳，直指人心，見性成佛」：是指出禪的立宗的基礎及體驗的方法。既是「教外別傳」，故無所依之經典；既「不立文字」，故亦無由以見理論的構想；祇以「見性」一事，為「成佛」之道而已。所以古人說：「禪宜默不宜說」；或謂「禪之一字，非聖凡所測」。

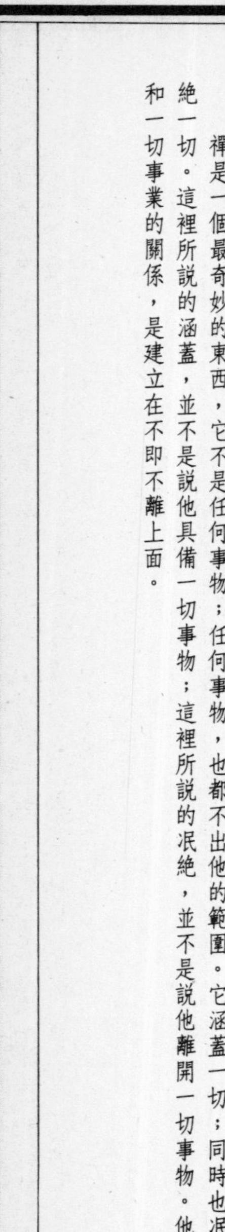
禪是一個最奇妙的東西，它不是任何事物；任何事物，也都不出他的範圍。它涵蓋一切；同時也泯絕一切。這裡所說的涵蓋，並不是說他具備一切事物；這裡所說的泯絕，並不是說他離開一切事物。他和一切事業的關係，是建立在不即不離上面。

WHAT IS ZEN?

A BABY FISH ONCE ASKED AN ELDER FISH:

I KEEP HEARING PEOPLE TALK ABOUT THIS THING CALLED THE SEA. JUST WHAT *IS* THE SEA?

THE SEA IS WHAT SURROUNDS YOU.

BUT WHY CAN'T I SEE IT?

THE SEA IS WITHIN YOU AND ALL AROUND YOU. YOU WERE BORN IN THE SEA AND WILL DIE IN THE SEA. THE SEA ENVELOPS YOU, JUST LIKE YOUR OWN SKIN DOES.

CONFUCIUS SAID, "FISH FORGET THAT THEY LIVE IN LAKES AND RIVERS; PEOPLE FORGET THAT THEY LIVE IN THE MAGIC OF THE DAO." PEOPLE LIVE IN A SEA OF ZEN, YET THEY DON'T KNOW WHAT IT IS. WOULD YOU LIKE TO KNOW WHAT ZEN IS?

PLEASE, READ ON...

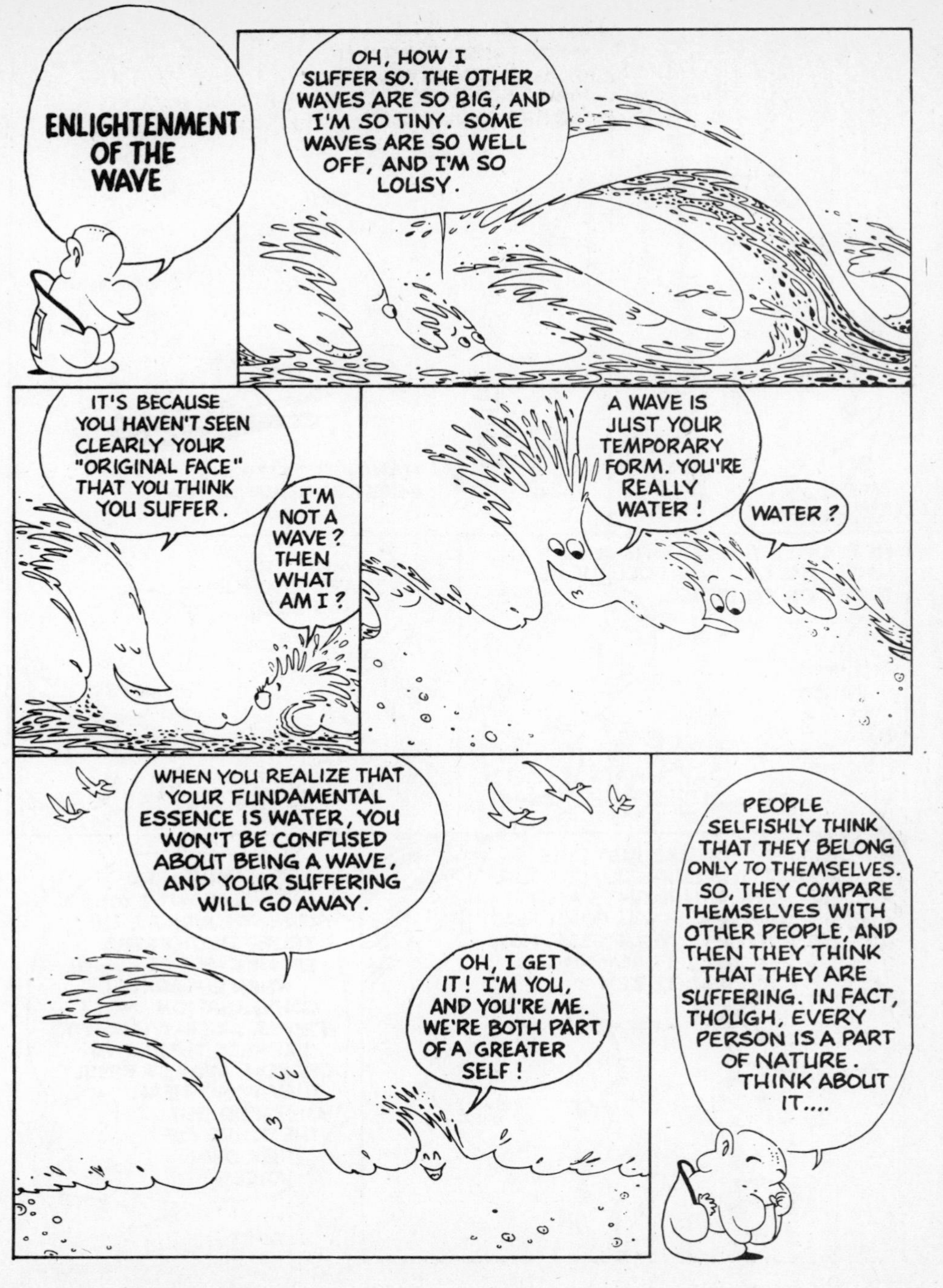

現代的科學，在外形上，得區別人類與其他的存在物，可是談到內面的存在，可說便是不能認清彼此的區別了。所以在禪觀物，把萬有生命的「法性」與人類的「佛性」，祇就自覺的有無方面而標異其名，至於本質，便沒有什麼不同，故從這一元的立場成立萬物一體觀，是不應強劃分其區別的。

南隱是日本明治時代（一八六八——一九一二）的一位禪師。有一天，有位大學教授來向他問禪，他只以茶相待。他將茶水注入這位來賓的杯中，直到杯滿，而後又繼續注入。

這位教授眼睜睜地望着茶水不息地溢出杯外，直到再也不能沉默下去了，終於説道：「已經漫出來了，不要再倒了！」「你就像這隻杯子一樣，」南隱答道：「裏面裝滿了你自己的看法和想法。你不先把你自己的杯子空掉，叫我如何對你説禪？」

THE OUTCOME OF ENLIGHTENMENT
EVER SINCE ANCIENT TIMES, MANY PEOPLE HAVE LEFT THEIR HOMES AND LOVED ONES TO ENTER THE GATES OF BUDDHISM AND STUDY ZEN MEDITATION.
THEY EXPEND A GREAT AMOUNT OF TIME AND ENERGY IN DISCIPLINED CONTEMPLATIVE TRAINING, BUT WHAT IS IT THAT THEY GAIN?
IF THIS QUESTION WERE POSED TO ENLIGHTENED ZEN MASTERS, THEY WOULD MOST LIKELY ANSWER:
NOTHING
WHEN WE STOP DIFFERENTIATING, HALT OUR DELUSIONS, AND PUT AN END TO ALL THOUGHTS, THE TWO HINDRANCES OF DISCURSIVE THOUGHT AND INTENTION WILL DISSOLVE, AND AS OUR MINDS FILL WITH PEACE, THERE WILL BE "NOTHING" WE WON'T UNDERSTAND.

無字，是參禪的人首先應該透過的關門，是佛性開顯的第一步。因有了這一步的飛躍，纔得打開涅槃的妙境；可是這必須的要件，不是學說的研究，祇是窮迫向自己的心路；要心路絕處，那就不可不驀直地精進努力纔得。

所以禪是把有無、凡聖、迷悟等的概念一切拋下，而入於無的三昧，使心成「無化」；一達到無的極致時，真如識自然自內發動起來，因之觸着這發動的妙機。

據禪的立場說：宇宙間的東西，都是獨自存在，沒有對立的，一切都是超對立的存在。所以生也、死也，原是一樣；既沒與生相對的死，也沒有與死相對的生，這就是「生死即涅槃」的意思。

離了一切對立，即是實相的境地，在這裡，開始從根本主體上出現活動，創造新生命；於是真法，真智，真性，在這裡顯現。

If one engages in self-cultivation with the desire to sever the roots of defilement and erroneous thinking, it is not only to attain the tranquil realm of true emptiness which involves no-thought, no-idea, no-mind, no-self, etc.; it is also in pursuit of the wonderful wisdom that is experienced in and grows from a way of life that is different from the ordinary.

In that realm, the whole world is seen from one perspective, and there are no dichotomies; it is the true world where the self and others, as well as good and evil, are all transcended. "In confusion, the three realms exist; after enlightenment, the ten directions are empty." But how do we attain the realm of nothingness and emptiness?

ZEN SPEAKS

Shouts of Nothingness

慧能大師對「禪」有如下解釋：「何名禪定？外離相為禪，內不亂為定。外若著相，內心即亂。本性自淨自定。只為見境思境即亂。若見諸境心不亂者，是真定也。善知識！外離相即禪，內不亂即定。外禪內定，是為禪定。」慧能認為心始終不着於外相（即心不去追逐外境及內意識的事物），時時呈現出一種安詳與寧靜的喜悅與自由，這就是禪的最基本含義。

世尊昔在靈山會上拈華示衆，衆皆默然，惟迦葉尊者破顏微笑。世尊云：「吾有正法眼藏，涅槃妙心，實相無相微妙法門，不立文字，教外別傳，付囑摩訶迦葉。」

無門曰：黃面瞿曇傍若無人，壓良為賤，懸羊頭賣狗肉，將謂多少奇特。只如當時大衆都笑，正法眼藏作麼生傳？設使迦葉不笑，正法眼藏又作麼生傳？若道正法眼藏有傳授，黃面老子誑謼閭閻；若道無傳授，為甚麼獨許迦葉？頌曰：拈起花來，尾巴已露。迦葉破顏，人天罔措！

◉迦葉尊者，即摩訶迦葉，禪宗印度法系的第一祖。

◉實相本無相，可是拈起花來，已露形相，所以説已洩天機，露了尾巴。在這裏便不能在拈花處大做文章，應該想想花未拈起前，是什麼樣的境界？

◉迦葉這一破顏而笑，使得所有的天、人都罔然不知。因為迦葉何所見而笑，只有迦葉自己知道。這只許自知，乃是正法眼藏，涅槃妙心，不是文字語言所能表達的。不過迦葉的這一笑，也已有了相，如果後人都學迦葉的破顏，禪宗豈不變成了一場鬧劇？（以上節自吳怡「公案禪語」）

諸經論中，對於破時破空的文字特別多。如華嚴經云：「以一劫為一切劫，以一切劫為一劫(時)。以一切剎為一剎，以一剎為一切剎（空）」。維摩詰經云：「以四大海水入一毛孔，斷取三千大千世界，如陶家輪，著右掌中（空）。演七日以為一劫，促一劫以為七日（時）」。都是一方面破時，一方面破空。

迦葉因阿難問：「世尊傳金襴袈裟外，別傳何物？」葉喚云：「阿難！」難應：「諾！」葉云：「倒却門前刹竿著！」

無門曰：若向者裏下得一轉語親切，便見靈山一會儼然未散。其或未然：毘婆尸佛早留心，直至而今不得妙！頌曰：問處何如答處親？幾人於此眼生筋？兄呼弟應揚家醜，不屬陰陽別是春！

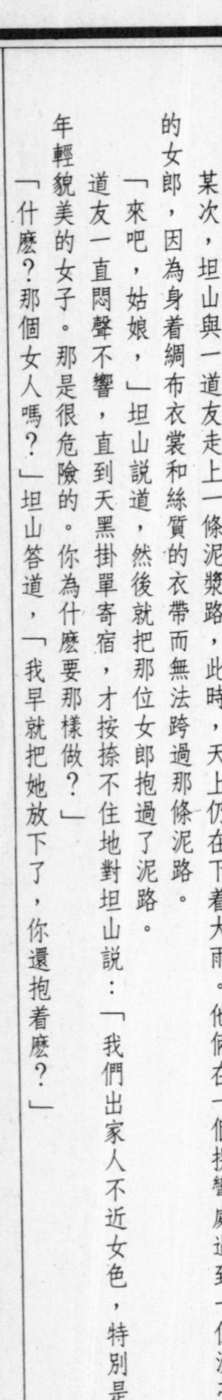

某次，坦山與一道友走上一條泥漿路，此時，天上仍在下着大雨。他倆在一個拐彎處遇到一位漂亮的女郎，因為身着綢布衣裳和絲質的衣帶而無法跨過那條泥路。

「來吧，姑娘，」坦山說道，然後就把那位女郎抱過了泥路。

道友一直悶聲不響，直到天黑掛單寄宿，才按捺不住地對坦山說：「我們出家人不近女色，特別是年輕貌美的女子。那是很危險的。你為什麼要那樣做？」

「什麼？那個女人嗎？」坦山答道，「我早就把她放下了，你還抱着麼？」

CARRYING A WOMAN ACROSS A RIVER

ONE DAY WHILE THE ZEN MONK TANZAN AND A YOUNG MONK WERE TRAVELLING, THEY HAPPENED UPON A BEAUTIFUL YOUNG LADY IN DISTRESS.

HERE, LET ME CARRY YOU ACROSS.

THANK YOU VERY MUCH. GOOD-BYE!

THE TWO CONTINUED ON THEIR JOURNEY FOR MORE THAN HALF A DAY....

I THOUGHT WE MONKS WERE SUPPOSED TO AVOID WOMEN. WHY DID YOU JUST DO THAT?

HUH? OH, YOU MEAN THAT WOMAN WAY BACK THERE?

I PUT HER DOWN LONG AGO. ARE YOU STILL CARRYING HER?

!

TANZAN CARRIED A PERSON ACROSS A RIVER, BUT IN HIS MIND HE WASN'T CARRYING A WOMAN; HE WAS COMPLETELY DETACHED AND HAD NO MISGIVINGS. THE ONE WHO WAS REALLY CARRYING A WOMAN SEEMS TO HAVE BEEN THE YOUNGER MONK, WOULDN'T YOU SAY?

衆生自無始以來，生活方式與生活環境，各有不同。故習染亦有差異。因此對於同一事物，各有不同的觀點。但其動機則一，那就是我執觀念。只要是與自己利害有關的，便立即表現出來。佛家將這種本能的意識活動，稱為無明。斷習就是要斷掉無明。魚朝恩問慧忠國師曰：「何者是無明，無明從何時起」？師曰：「佛法衰相今現，奴也解問佛法」。此語對魚朝恩當然是一種侮辱。魚朝恩當時勃然變色。師曰：「此是無明，無明從此起」。魚朝恩當即有省。

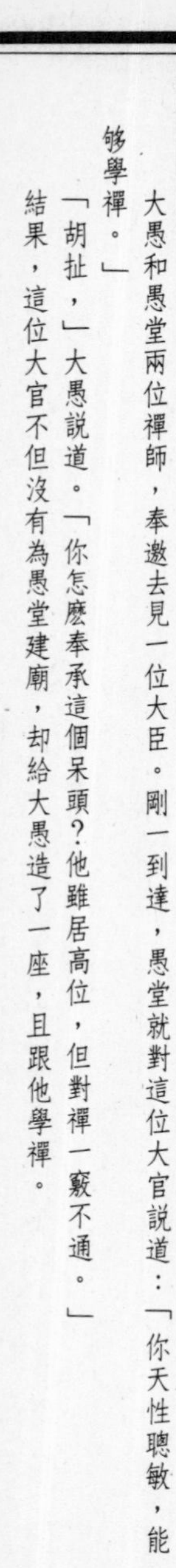
大愚和愚堂兩位禪師，奉邀去見一位大臣。剛一到達，愚堂就對這位大官説道：「你天性聰敏，能够學禪。」

「胡扯，」大愚説道。「你怎麼奉承這個呆頭？他雖居高位，但對禪一竅不通。」

結果，這位大官不但沒有為愚堂建廟，却給大愚造了一座，且跟他學禪。

THE LAMEBRAIN OFFICIAL

THE ZEN MASTERS DAYU AND YUTANG ACCEPTED AN INVITATION TO INSTRUCT A MAJOR OFFICIAL INTERESTED IN ZEN.

YOU ARE A NATURALLY INTELLIGENT AND RECEPTIVE MAN. I THINK YOU WILL MAKE A FINE STUDENT OF ZEN.

YOU'VE GOT TO BE KIDDING! THIS LAMEBRAIN MAY HAVE A HIGH POSITION, BUT HE WOULDN'T KNOW ZEN IF HE WERE HIT OVER THE HEAD WITH IT!

AFTER LISTENING TO YOUR TWO HONORABLE OPINIONS, I HAVE DECIDED WHAT TO DO.

IN THE END, NOT ONLY DID THE OFFICIAL NOT BUILD A TEMPLE FOR YUTANG, HE BUILT ONE FOR DAYU INSTEAD AND STUDIED ZEN WITH HIM.

DISREGARDING THE HIGH POSITION OF THE OFFICIAL, DAYU SPOKE EXACTLY WHAT WAS ON HIS MIND, AND AS A RESULT WAS HELD IN HIGH REGARD FOR IT. WHEN THE DUALISM OF GOOD AND BAD IS GONE FROM YOUR MIND, ONLY THEN WILL YOU BE NEARING ZEN.

在一切差別相中，只要我們有超越物我，超越自他的理念。就能證得真我。佛是乾矢橛，佛是蔴三斤。是從乾矢橛中和蔴三斤中悟得佛性。有超越感的，處處是佛。

六祖有一次向大衆說：「我這裡有一個東西，無頭無尾，無名無字，無背無面，你們是否認識呢」？神會答道：「他是諸佛的本源，神會的佛性」。六祖說：「我已告訴你是無名無字的，你偏要叫他作本源和佛性。將來你有一間蓋頭的茅屋，也只是一個知解宗徒」。自性一落知解，便變成識心中的事物。宗門禪的特點，是「教外別傳，不立文字」。所以有了知解，便與不立文字的宗旨不符。向居士云：「無名作名，因其名則是非生矣。無理作理，因其理則爭論起矣」。（引自周中一「禪話」）

THE ORDER OF LIFE AND DEATH
THERE WAS ONCE A WEALTHY MAN WHO ASKED THE ZEN MONK SENGAI TO CREATE A WORK OF CALLIGRAPHY FOR HIM....
FATHER DIES SON DIES GRANDSON DIES
— SENGAI
AAAH!
I WANTED YOU TO WRITE SOMETHING AUSPICIOUS! WHAT ARE YOU TRYING TO PULL?
THIS **IS** AUSPICIOUS.
IF YOUR SONS WERE TO DIE BEFORE YOU, OR IF YOUR GRANDSONS WERE TO DIE BEFORE YOUR SONS, YOU WOULD BE EXTREMELY UNHAPPY.
IF THE PEOPLE IN YOUR FAMILY LIVE GENERATION AFTER GENERATION AND DIE ACCORDING TO THIS ORDER, WHAT IS MORE AUSPICIOUS THAN THAT?
THAT MAKES SENSE.
"LIFE IS TAXING, DEATH IS RELAXING" (ZHUANGZI). DEATH IS LIKE A WEARY TRAVELLER RETURNING HOME. ISN'T IT THE MOST FORTUNATE THING FOR EVERYONE TO DIE IN THEIR NATURAL ORDER?

禪家是以真我為主體，真我是不受軀殼的限制的。但人情上總覺得死是永恆的離開塵世，免不了悲哀。感情脆弱的人，往往承受不了這種悲哀的打擊。六祖臨終時，徒衆痛哭。他告訴大家：「我是另有去處，你們不必悲哀。」六祖是把生死一樣的看待，死不過是等於旅行途中換一個旅舍而已。自己既知道了去處，自可處之泰然。

在日本，禪宗尚未傳入之前，天臺宗的學者即已坐禪。那時有同學四人，非常要好，但為了避免閒扯打岔而好好用功打坐起見，他們約定：誓守不語戒七天。頭一天的白天，他們都靜默不語，故而打坐的效果也非常之好。但到了夜深之際，油燈忽明忽暗，眼看就要熄了。他們中的一位禁不住向侍從叫道：「請添些燈油！」另一位同學聽了頗以為怪。「我們應該一言不發的呀！」他說。

「你倆真蠢，」另一位同學說道，「為什麼偏要講話呢?!」

「只有我沒有講話！」第四位同學應道。

山岡鐵舟到處參訪名師。一天，他見了相國寺的獨園和尚。為了表示他的悟境，他頗為得意地對獨園説道：「心、佛、以及衆生，三者皆空。現象的真性是空。無悟、無迷、無聖、無凡、無施、無受。」

當時獨園正在抽煙，未曾答腔。但他突然舉起煙管將山岡打了一下，使得這位年輕的禪者至為憤怒。

「一切皆空，」獨園問道，「哪兒來這麼大的脾氣？」

楊黼離別雙親到四川去拜訪無際菩薩，在路上碰到了一個老和尚，那和尚問他：「你去那裏」？楊黼告訴對方他要去做無際的學生，老和尚便說：「與其去找菩薩，還不如去找佛」。楊黼問：「那裏有佛啊」！老和尚回答：「你回家時，看到有個人披着毯子，穿反了鞋來迎接你，記住，那就是佛」。

楊黼依照吩咐回家，在抵家的那天，已是深夜，他的母親已睡覺了，一聽到兒子叫門，高興得來不及穿衣，便披上毯子當外衣，匆忙中，拖鞋也穿錯了脚，趕緊來迎接兒子，楊黼一看到母親這種情形，立刻大悟，此後他便專心侍奉雙親，並寫了一大部的孝經註。

師自黃梅得法，回至韶州曹侯村，人無知者，時有儒士劉志略，禮遇甚厚。志略有姑為尼，名「無盡藏」，常誦「大涅槃經」。師暫聽，即知妙義，遂為解說。尼乃執卷問字。師曰：「字即不識，義即請問。」尼曰：「字尚不識，焉能會義。」師曰：「諸佛妙理，非關文字。」尼驚異之。遍告里中耆德云：「此是有道之士，宜請供養。」有魏武侯玄孫曹叔良及居民，競來瞻禮。

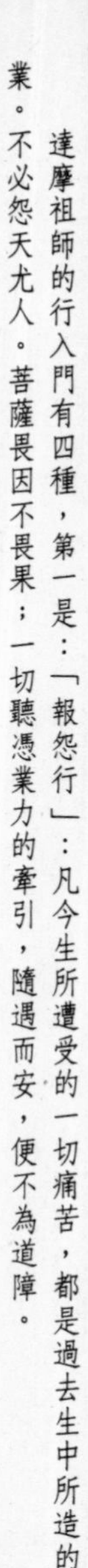
達摩祖師的行入門有四種，第一是：「報怨行」：凡今生所遭受的一切痛苦，都是過去生中所造的業。不必怨天尤人。菩薩畏因不畏果；一切聽憑業力的牽引，隨遇而安，便不為道障。

THE LOST STUDENT

ONE DAY WHILE THE ZEN MASTER BANKEI WAS GIVING A LECTURE, A DISCIPLE SUDDENLY STOOD UP AND YELLED OUT....

AH-HA! CAUGHT YOU FILCHING MONEY AGAIN!

YOU LITTLE...!

FORGIVE HIM!

NO WAY! WE'VE FORGIVEN HIM EVERY TIME, AND HE JUST KEEPS ON STEALING.

YEA! IF YOU DON'T KICK HIM OUT THIS TIME, WE'LL ALL LEAVE.

YOU ARE ALL PERCEPTIVE STUDENTS AND UNDERSTAND THE DIFFERENCE BETWEEN RIGHT AND WRONG. HE IS THE ONLY ONE WHO DOESN'T UNDERSTAND EVEN THIS. IF I DON'T TEACH HIM, WHO WILL?

I AM GOING TO LET HIM STAY HERE EVEN IF EVERY ONE OF YOU LEAVES.

AT THIS, THE PICKPOCKET MONK FELL TO HIS KNEES AND PROMISED TO REFORM, SUDDENLY UNDERSTANDING RIGHT AND WRONG, GOOD AND BAD.

IF YOU HAD ONE HUNDRED SHEEP AND ONE OF THEM LOST ITS WAY, WOULDN'T YOU IMMEDIATELY GO IN SEARCH OF THE LOST ONE, ABANDONING THE OTHER NINETY-NINE IN THE OPEN FIELDS? IT IS IMPORTANT TO HELP THOSE WHO NEED HELP THE MOST.

一天晚上，七里禪師正在誦經之時，一名強盜帶着一把尖刀進來向他表示：要不拿錢出來，要不就要他的老命。七里對他說道：「不要打擾我。錢在那個抽屜裏，你自己去拿。」說罷繼續誦經。

這個闖入者拿了他大部份的錢，正要走開。「收人家禮物應該說聲謝謝，」七里說道。那人向他致謝後立即走了開去。數天之後，這個強盜被捕了，他招認搶竊多處，受害人中包含有七里在內。當七里被召作證時，他說：「此人不是強盜，至少，據我所知確是如此。錢是我給他的，他已謝過我了。」

此人服刑期滿後即來叩見七里，求他收為徒弟。

自性是不分時間與空間而充塞宇宙的。我們無法用六根去接觸到他。語言是由意根與舌根所產生的；代表語言的文字，也是在意根指揮之下，用手描畫出來的。都是只能表詮現象界的事物，不能表詮超越現象的自性。

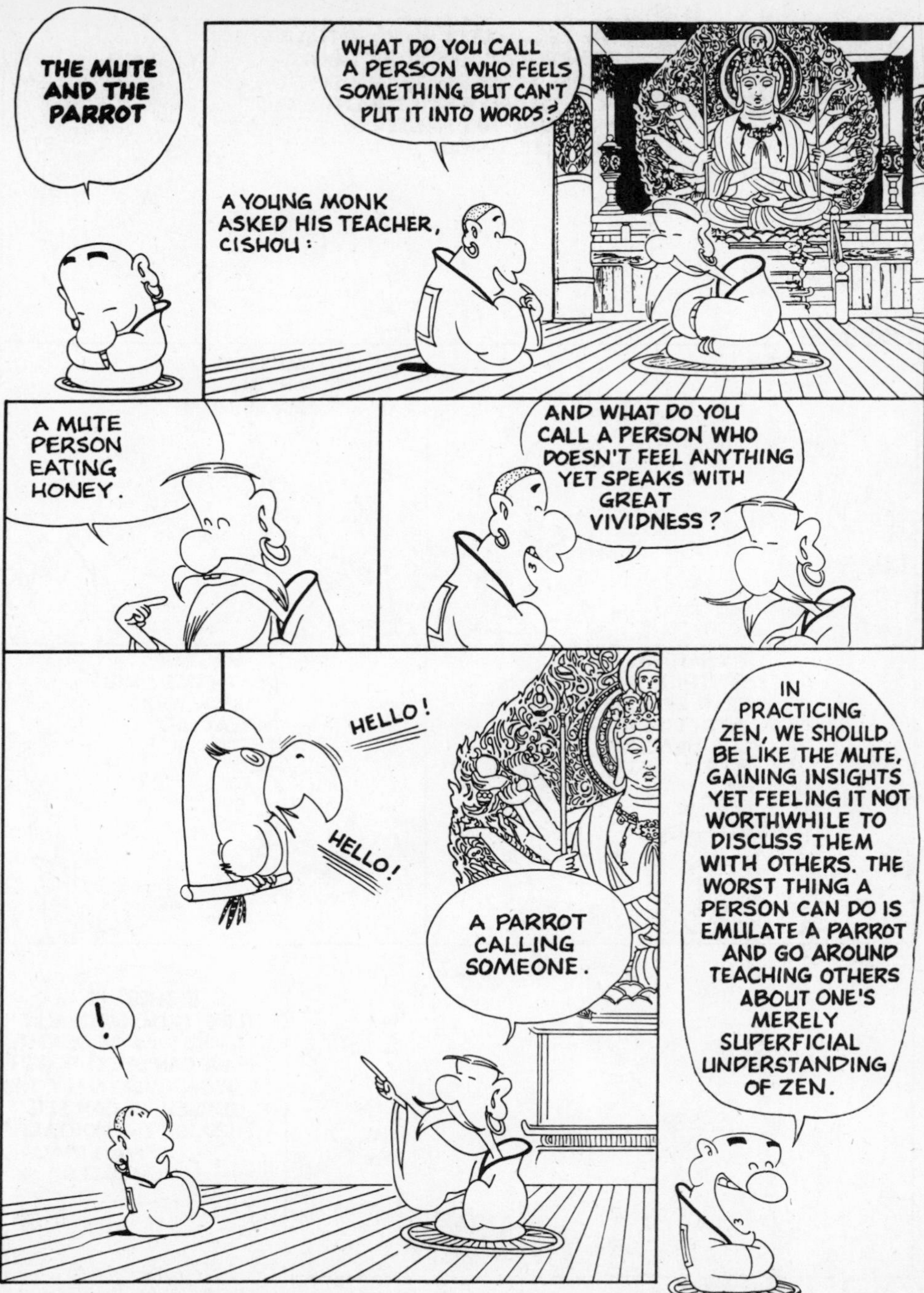

慧林慈受有如下面一段對話：

和尚問：「當一個人感覺到而說不出，他像什麼」？慈受說：「他像啞子吃蜜」。和尚問：「當一個人並沒有感覺到，却談得有聲有色，他像什麼」？慈受說：「他像鸚鵡叫人」。

禪宗要我們學習啞子一樣，無論是苦、是甜，或是夢，都不足與外人道。最犯忌的就是像鸚鵡一樣，心中毫無所得，只在嘴巴上亂說，而流於文字禪，口頭禪。(引自吳經熊著吳怡譯「禪學的黃金時代」)

一休禪師自幼就很聰明。他的老師有一隻非常寶愛的茶杯，是件稀世之寶。一天，他無意中將它打破了，內心感到非常狼狽。但就在這時候，他聽到了老師的脚步聲，連忙把打破的茶杯藏在背後。當他的老師走到他面前時，他忽然開口問道：「人為什麼一定要死呢？」

「這是自然之事，」他的老師答道，「世間的一切，有生就有死。」

這時，一休拿出打破的茶杯接着說道：「你的茶杯死期到了！」

契冲是明治時代的大師之一，曾任京都大教堂東福寺的管長多年。一天，京都總督首次造訪，他的侍者將有「京都總督北垣」數字的名片送到他的面前。

「我與這個傢伙沒有瓜葛，」契冲對他的侍者説道。「叫他出去！」侍者送回名片，表示歉意。「那是我的錯誤，」總督説道，用筆將「京都總督」四字塗掉。「煩請再問你的老師。」

「噢，是北垣啊！」這位大師看了名片説道。「我要見見這個傢伙！」

佛教旨在為人解決痛苦，釋尊因此而離家。人常以自我為中心去看事物，若事與願違，則難免心生苦痛。

事物乃由緣起、變化、空、無我、不污染等要素構成。但是，自己被污染、固執、反抗命運、與人爭奪、好與人比較等，或只站在自私的立場去衡量他人，皆是痛苦的元凶。

會對不污染的事實（真理）產生共鳴，就能捨去自我為主的觀念，以無我去面對他人，如此使自己

SELF AND OTHER
THERE WAS A CERTAIN ARMY DOCTOR WHOSE JOB IT WAS TO ACCOMPANY SOLDIERS TO BATTLE AND TEND TO THEIR WOUNDS ON THE BATTLEFIELD....
BUT IT SEEMED LIKE EVERY TIME HE PATCHED SOMEONE UP, THE SOLDIER WOULD JUST GO RIGHT BACK INTO BATTLE AND END UP BEING KILLED....
AFTER THIS HAD HAPPENED OVER AND OVER AGAIN, THE DOCTOR FINALLY BROKE DOWN....
IF IT'S THEIR FATE TO DIE, WHY SHOULD I TRY TO SAVE THEM ? IF MY MEDICINE MEANS ANYTHING, THEN WHY DO THEY GO BACK TO WAR AND GET KILLED ?

配合真理並為之同化，這才是佛教的目的。

別把它當成知識或理論，只當是自己的心態，而將自己溶入事實（真實），這需要有心之突破的體驗才行。

但人們對自己的身體、心、習慣、經驗等，都有既成的想法，幾乎不能用無我的眼光，去看事物的真相，即使自以為很認真地看，事實上却看不見。甚至根本沒有站在事物的立場，去思考的經驗，此乃因尚未脱離軀殼的緣故。

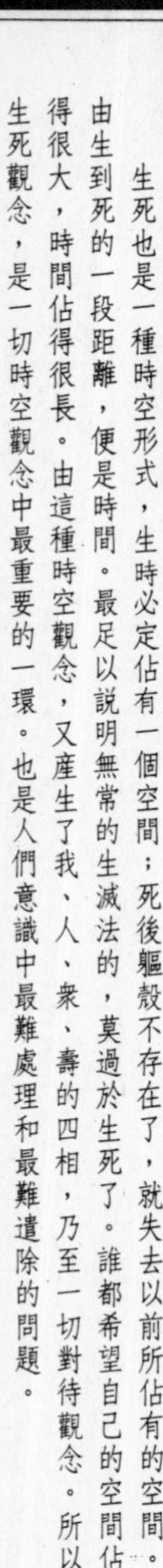

生死也是一種時空形式，生時必定佔有一個空間；死後軀殼不存在了，就失去以前所佔有的空間。由生到死的一段距離，便是時間。最足以說明無常的生滅法的，莫過於生死了。誰都希望自己的空間佔得很大，時間佔得很長。由這種時空觀念，又產生了我、人、衆、壽的四相，乃至一切對待觀念。所以生死觀念，是一切時空觀念中最重要的一環。也是人們意識中最難處理和最難遣除的問題。

WORDS EXCEEDING ACTIONS

THERE WAS ONCE A WEALTHY OLD WOMAN WHO OFTEN WENT TO THE TEMPLE TO BURN INCENSE AND PRAY. KNEELING IN FRONT OF THE BUDDHA, SHE WOULD ALWAYS SAY:

I'VE LIVED A LONG LIFE, AND I AM READY WHENEVER YOU WOULD LIKE TO COME FOR ME. PRAISE TO AMITĀBHA.

LET'S HAVE SOME FUN WITH HER.

I'VE LIVED A LONG LIFE, AND I AM READY WHENEVER YOU WOULD LIKE TO COME FOR ME. PRAISE TO AMITĀBHA.

HEE-HEE

OLD WOMAN, TONIGHT IS THE NIGHT.

THE OLD WOMAN WAS TERRIBLY FRIGHTENED BY THIS AND DIED RIGHT THERE FROM THE SHOCK.

OH, NO!

COLORFUL AND INSPIRING WORDS WILL LOSE THEIR SIMPLICITY AND CAUSE CONFUSION. CONSISTENCY BETWEEN ACTIONS AND WORDS IS THE FOUNDATION OF SELF-CULTIVATION.

SOUND OF THE HOLLOW
THERE WAS ONCE A BUDDHIST MAN WHO WENT INTO THE MOUNTAINS IN SEARCH OF A ZEN MASTER WHO COULD TAKE HIM THROUGH THE GATES OF ZEN.
ON YOUR WAY HERE, YOU PASSED THROUGH A HOLLOW, DID YOU NOT?
YES, I DID.
DID YOU HEAR THE SOUND OF THE HOLLOW?
YES, I DID.
THE PLACE WHERE YOU HEARD THE SOUND OF THE HOLLOW IS WHERE THE PATH THAT LEADS TO THE GATES OF ZEN BEGINS.
!
THERE IS GOODNESS IN A BLOSSOMING FLOWER, AND THERE IS BEAUTY IN A WITHERING FLOWER. WHEN YOU CAN SEE THE BEAUTY AND GOODNESS IN EVERYTHING AROUND YOU, YOU HAVE ENTERED THE GATES OF ZEN.

問：「學人乍入叢林，乞師指箇入路」。師（玄沙）曰：「還聞偃溪水聲否」？曰：「聞」。師曰：「是汝入處」。

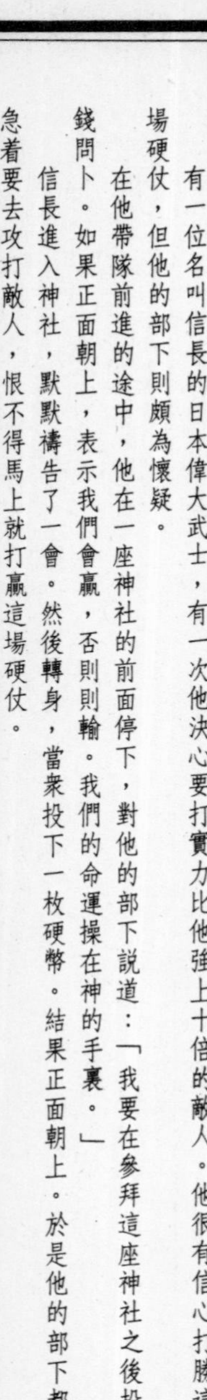

有一位名叫信長的日本偉大武士，有一次他決心要打實力比他強上十倍的敵人。他很有信心打勝這場硬仗，但他的部下則頗為懷疑。

在他帶隊前進的途中，他在一座神社的前面停下，對他的部下說道：「我要在參拜這座神社之後投錢問卜。如果正面朝上，表示我們會贏，否則則輸。我們的命運操在神的手裏。」

信長進入神社，默默禱告了一會。然後轉身，當衆投下一枚硬幣。結果正面朝上。於是他的部下都急着要去攻打敵人，恨不得馬上就打贏這場硬仗。

FATE IS IN YOUR OWN HANDS

IN ANCIENT TIMES, THERE WAS A GENERAL WHO WAS ABOUT TO LEAD HIS TROOPS INTO BATTLE AGAINST AN ENEMY ARMY TEN TIMES THE SIZE OF HIS OWN.

ALONG THE WAY, HE STOPPED AT A SMALL ROADSIDE ALTAR TO PRAY.

I'M NOW GOING TO USE THIS COIN TO PREDICT OUR FATE. IF IT'S HEADS, WE'LL WIN. IF IT'S TAILS, WE'LL LOSE.

OUR FATE IS IN THE HANDS OF THE GODS!

「誰也不能改變命運的掌握，」打勝之後，他的一位隨從説道。

「誠然如此，」信長説道，説着抖出一枚硬幣，兩面都是正面。

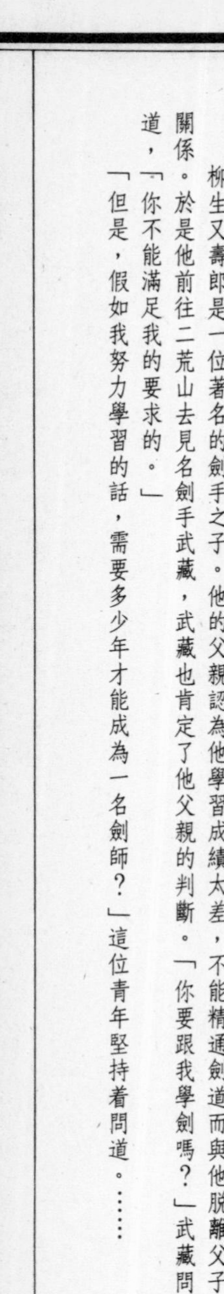
柳生又壽郎是一位著名的劍手之子。他的父親認為他學習成績太差，不能精通劍道而與他脫離父子關係。於是他前往二荒山去見名劍手武藏，武藏也肯定了他父親的判斷。「你要跟我學劍嗎？」武藏問道，「你不能滿足我的要求的。」

「但是，假如我努力學習的話，需要多少年才能成為一名劍師？」這位青年堅持着問道。……

THE FASTER THE SLOWER

AN EAGER STUDENT ASCENDED THE MOUNTAINS TO STUDY THE ART OF SWORDFIGHTING UNDER A GREAT MASTER.

MASTER, IF I STUDY DILIGENTLY, HOW LONG WILL IT TAKE ME TO LEARN THE SKILLS OF SWORD-FIGHTING?

TEN YEARS, PERHAPS.

MY FATHER IS AN OLD MAN, AND I MUST RETURN TO LOOK AFTER HIM. WHAT IF I WORK EXCEPTIONALLY HARD, THEN HOW LONG WILL IT TAKE ME?

IN THAT CASE, IT WILL PROBABLY TAKE THIRTY YEARS.

!

FIRST YOU SAID TEN YEARS AND NOW YOU SAY THIRTY... LOOK, I'M WILLING TO SUFFER ANY KIND OF HARDSHIP AND SACRIFICE. I JUST WANT TO LEARN IT IN THE SHORTEST TIME POSSIBLE.

IN THAT CASE, YOU'LL HAVE TO STUDY WITH ME FOR SEVENTY YEARS.

!

IF WE TAKE OUR TIME, WE'LL ACHIEVE OUR GOALS FASTER THAN IF WE HURRY. THIS IS WHAT IS MEANT BY "THE ORDINARY MIND IS THE DAO."

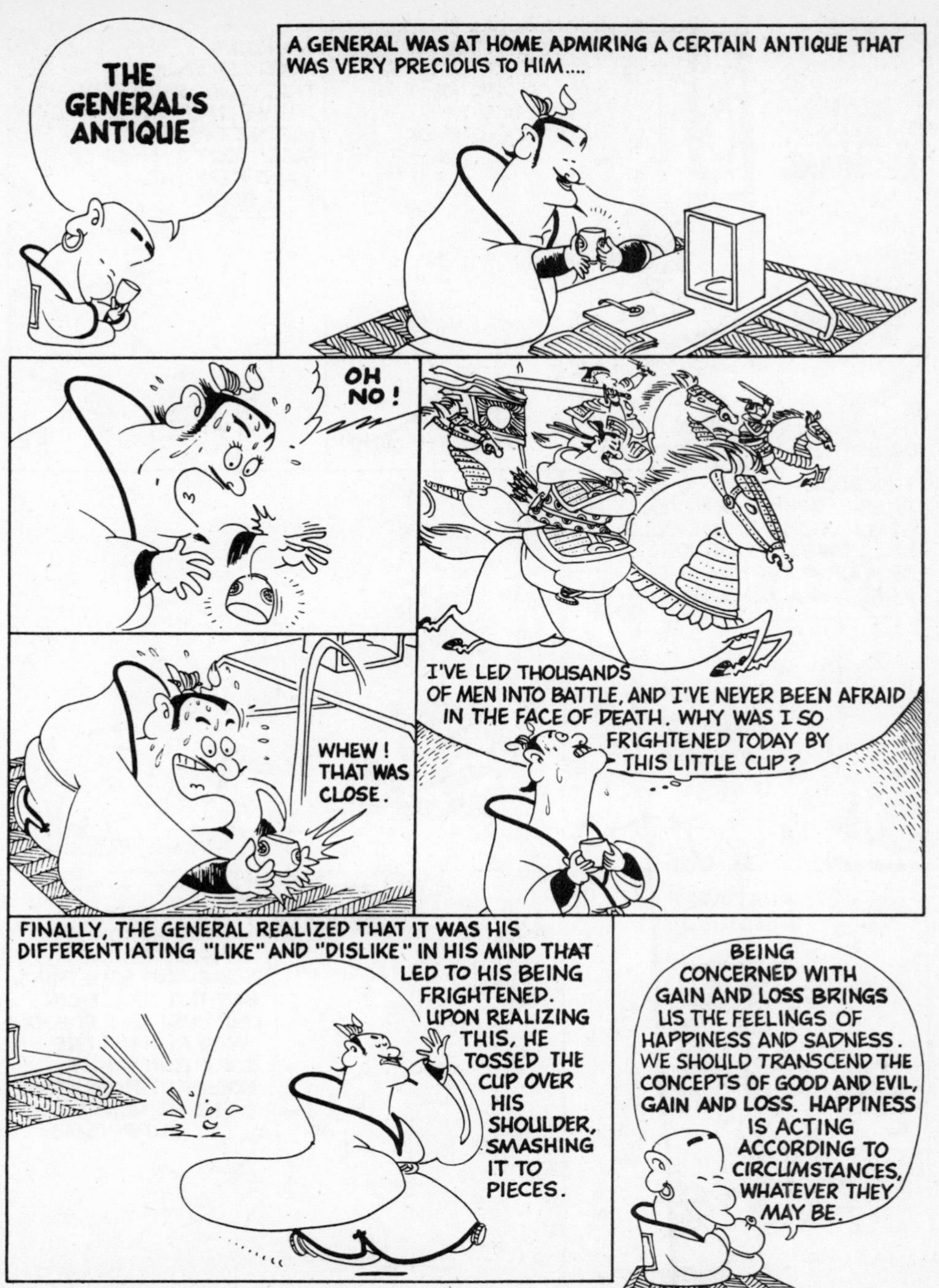

大道即是「只要無憎愛，即可洞然明白」。所謂的洞然又是什麼呢？洞然就是沒有障礙。若細觀日常生活，則到處都充滿障礙。障與礙是同樣的東西，都是礙手礙脚的意思。但為何又會發生礙手礙脚呢？這是由於自己有喜好與厭惡的緣故。

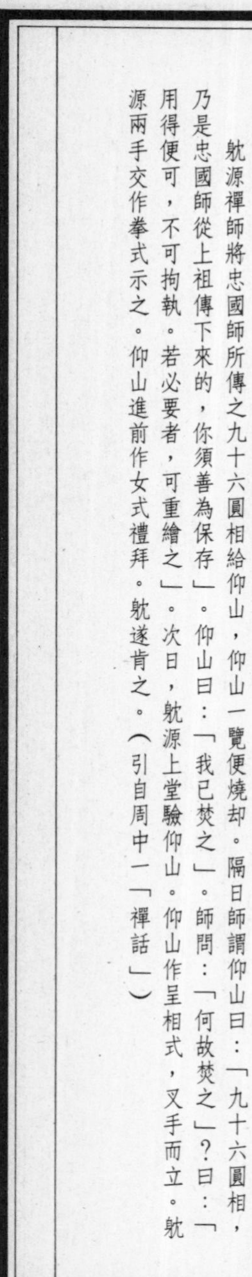

躭源禪師將忠國師所傳之九十六圓相給仰山，仰山一覽便燒却。隔日師謂仰山曰：「九十六圓相，乃是忠國師從上祖傳下來的，你須善為保存」。仰山曰：「我已焚之」。師問：「何故焚之」？曰：「用得便可，不可拘執。若必要者，可重繪之」。次日，躭源上堂驗仰山。仰山作呈相式，叉手而立。躭源兩手交作拳式示之。仰山進前作女式禮拜。躭遂肯之。（引自周中一「禪話」）

GIVING AND RECEIVING

I'M GETTING OLD. TO SYMBOLIZE YOUR SUCCEEDING ME, I GIVE YOU THIS PRECIOUS BOOK.

NO, NO, NO. I HAVE ACCEPTED YOUR ZEN THAT IS NOT RELIANT ON THE WRITTEN WORD. I LIKE ITS ORIGINAL FACE. YOU GO AHEAD AND KEEP THE BOOK.

THIS BOOK HAS BEEN PASSED DOWN FOR SEVEN GENERATIONS. YOU SHOULD STILL TAKE IT AS A TOKEN OF YOUR ACCEPTING THE ROBE AND ALMS BOWL.

ALL RIGHT.

!

WHAT ARE YOU DOING ?!

WHAT ARE YOU SAYING ?!

KNOWLEDGE AND ACTION SHOULD BE ONE. PREACHING SOMETHING BUT NOT PRACTICING IT IS JUST LIKE SOMEONE WHO RECITES THE SCRIPTURES BUT DOESN'T UNDERSTAND THE PRINCIPLES OF BUDDHISM.

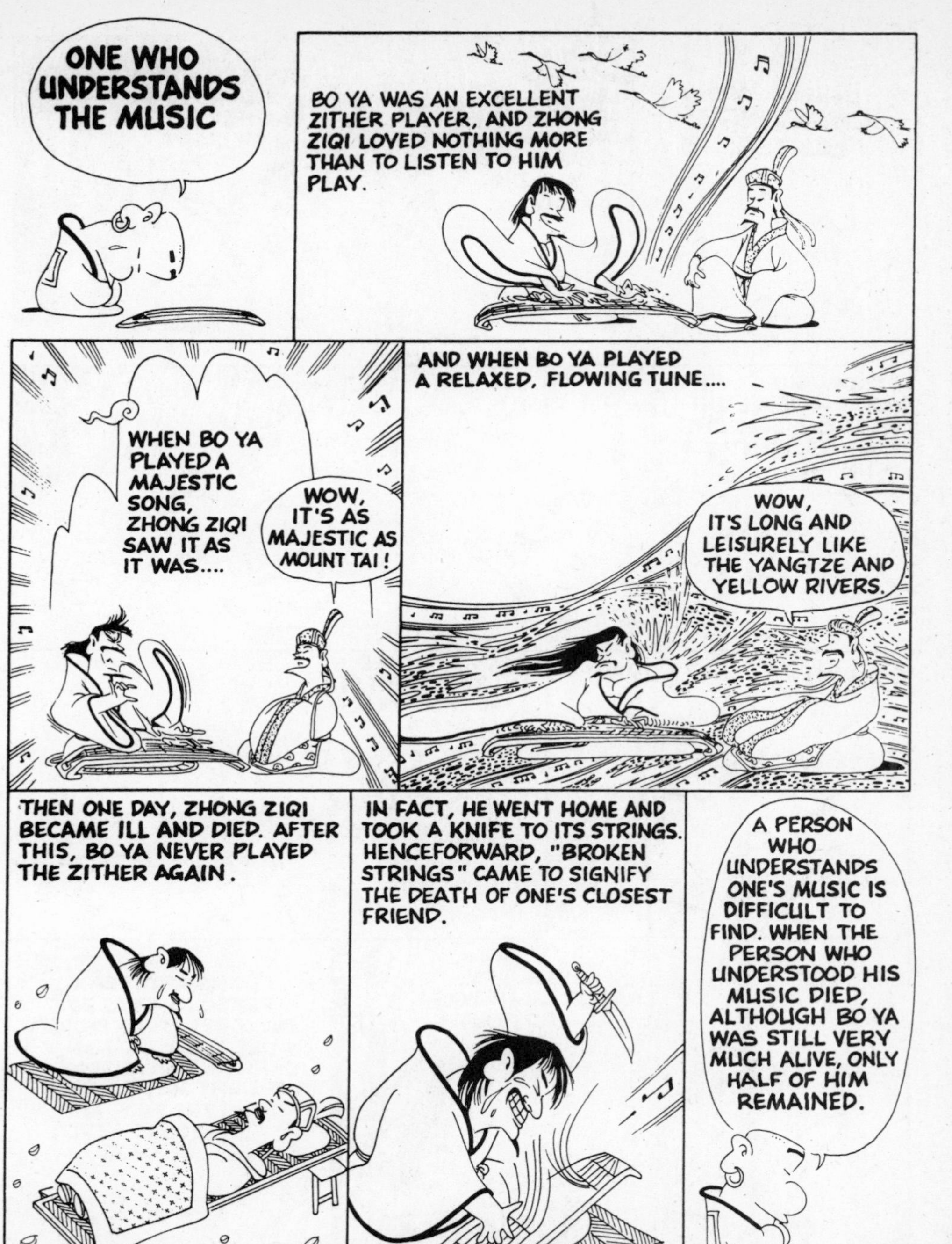

伯牙鼓琴，鍾子期聽之，方鼓琴，而志在太山，鍾子期曰：「善哉乎鼓琴，巍巍乎若太山。」少選之間，而志在流水，鍾子期又曰：「善哉乎鼓琴，湯湯乎若流水。」鍾子期死，伯牙破琴絶弦，終身不復鼓琴，以為世無足復為鼓琴者。

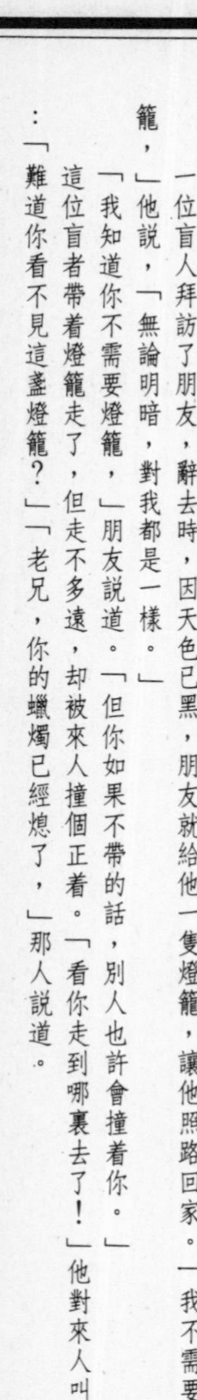

一位盲人拜訪了朋友，辭去時，因天色已黑，朋友就給他一隻燈籠，讓他照路回家。「我不需要燈籠，」他說，「無論明暗，對我都是一樣。」

「我知道你不需要燈籠，」朋友說道。「但你如果不帶的話，別人也許會撞着你。」

這位盲者帶着燈籠走了，但走不多遠，却被來人撞個正着。「看你走到哪裏去了！」他對來人叫道：「難道你看不見這盞燈籠？」「老兄，你的蠟燭已經熄了，」那人說道。

A BLIND MAN CARRYING A LANTERN

WHEN A BLIND MAN WAS LEAVING HIS FRIEND'S HOUSE, THE FRIEND HANDED HIM A LANTERN TO TAKE ON HIS WAY.

I DON'T NEED A LANTERN. IT'S ALL THE SAME TO ME WHETHER IT'S DARK OR LIGHT.

I KNOW, BUT IF YOU DON'T HAVE A LIGHT WITH YOU, SOMEONE MIGHT ACCIDENTALLY RUN INTO YOU.

OH, ALL RIGHT.

UMPH!

UMPH!

CAN'T YOU SEE A LIGHT RIGHT IN FRONT OF YOUR FACE?!

!

HEY, BUDDY, YOUR LIGHT WAS ALREADY OUT!

USING ANOTHER PERSON'S IDEAS TO ENLIGHTEN OTHER PEOPLE IS LIKE THE BLIND MAN CARRYING A LANTERN-- THE LIGHT MAY GO OUT ALONG THE WAY, AND YOU'LL NEVER KNOW.

良寬禪師居住在山脚下的一座小茅棚中，生活過得非常簡單。一天晚上，小偷光顧他的茅廬，結果發現沒有一樣東西值得一偷。

良寬從外面回來，碰見了這位老兄。「你也許是跋涉長途而來，」他對小偷説道，「不該空手而回。請把我身上的衣服當着禮物拿去吧。」小偷感到不知所云，拿了衣服就溜。

良寬赤着身子坐下看月。「可憐的傢伙，」他在心裏沉吟道，「可惜我不能把這美麗的月亮也送給他！」

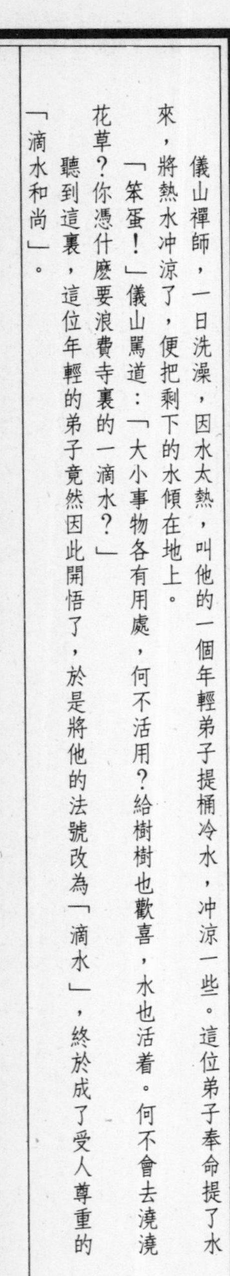
儀山禪師，一日洗澡，因水太熱，叫他的一個年輕弟子提桶冷水，冲涼一些。這位弟子奉命提了水來，將熱水冲涼了，便把剩下的水傾在地上。

「笨蛋！」儀山罵道：「大小事物各有用處，何不活用？給樹樹也歡喜，水也活着。何不會去澆澆花草？你憑什麼要浪費寺裏的一滴水？」

聽到這裏，這位年輕的弟子竟然因此開悟了，於是將他的法號改為「滴水」，終於成了受人尊重的「滴水和尚」。

A BLADE OF GRASS, A DROP OF DEW

MMM....THERE, THAT'S PERFECT.

ONE DAY WHILE THE ZEN MASTER YISHAN WAS TAKING A BATH, HIS BATHWATER WAS TOO HOT, SO HE ASKED HIS DISCIPLE TO ADD A LITTLE COLD WATER....

!

YOU IDIOT! EVERYTHING BIG AND SMALL HAS ITS USE. WHY DID YOU WASTE THAT? YOU COULD AT LEAST DUMP IT BY A TREE. A TREE WOULD WELCOME IT, AND THE WATER WOULD BE PUT TO GOOD USE.

WHY DIDN'T YOU DUMP IT IN THE FLOWER BED? WHY MUST YOU WASTE EVEN ONE DROP OF THE MONASTERY'S WATER?

THIS SCOLDING BROUGHT THE MONK TO ENLIGHTENMENT, AND FROM THAT DAY FORWARD, HE WENT BY THE NAME "DROP OF WATER."

EVERYTHING HAS ITS OWN USE. REGARDLESS OF SOME THINGS' SEEMING INSIGNIFICANCE, EVERYTHING HAS ITS PLACE IN NATURE.

當我們生理上失去平衡時，就有了痛、癢、勞、逸種種不同的感覺。得到平衡時，便失去一切感覺。心理上失去平衡時，便有喜、怒、哀、樂、善、惡、是、非的觀念。所謂動念即乖。一得到平衡，便一切都寂靜了。莊子所謂：「魚相忘乎江湖，人相忘乎道術」。便是一種平衡的境界。

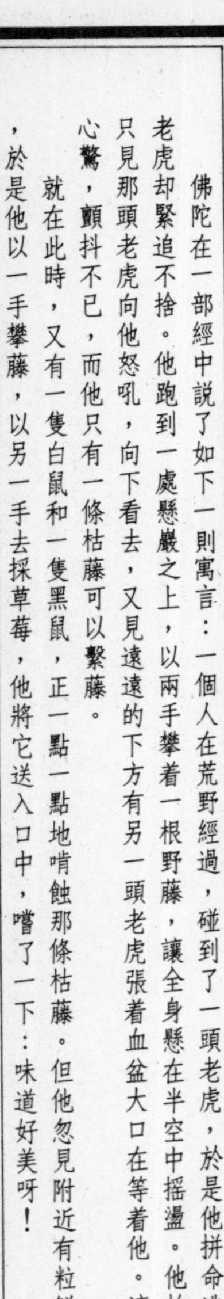
佛陀在一部經中說了如下一則寓言：一個人在荒野經過，碰到了一頭老虎，於是他拼命逃跑，但那老虎卻緊追不捨。他跑到一處懸巖之上，以兩手攀着一根野藤，讓全身懸在半空中搖盪。他抬頭仰望，只見那頭老虎向他怒吼，向下看去，又見遠遠的下方有另一頭老虎張着血盆大口在等着他。這使他膽戰心驚，顫抖不已，而他只有一條枯藤可以繫藤。

就在此時，又有一隻白鼠和一隻黑鼠，正一點一點地啃蝕那條枯藤。但他忽見附近有粒鮮美的草莓，於是他以一手攀藤，以另一手去採草莓，他將它送入口中，嚐了一下：味道好美呀！

PAST, PRESENT, FUTURE

ONE DAY WHILE WALKING THROUGH THE WILDERNESS, A MAN HAPPENED UPON A VICIOUS TIGER.

HELP!

HE RAN BUT SOON CAME TO THE EDGE OF A CLIFF. CLIMBING DOWN A VINE, HE DISCOVERED ANOTHER TIGER AT THE BOTTOM.

THEN TWO RATS APPEARED AND BEGAN GNAWING ON THE VINE....

RIP!

OH, NO!

SUDDENLY, HE NOTICED A PLUMP RED STRAWBERRY.

HE PLUCKED IT AND POPPED IT IN HIS MOUTH....

DELICIOUS!

DON'T DWELL ON THE PAST. DON'T WORRY ABOUT THE FUTURE. EXPERIENCE AND CHERISH THE MOMENT. HAPPINESS IS ACTING ACCORDING TO CIRCUMSTANCES, WHATEVER THEY MAY BE.

無我是佛家的一句很普遍的口號，也只有佛家才有。不僅是人與人之間，無自他的分別；乃至物我的分別，也一概掃除。換言之：就是無主體、客體之分。表達此一意義的，佛家有一個很特殊而又最是恰當的名相：就是「能所兩忘」，或者是稱「能所一如」。能是指能够自主的我，所是指我所接觸的一切事物，也就是我以外的一切的環境。凡是被六根所能接觸到的一切事物都是所。簡言之：能所便是主體和客體。「能所兩忘」，或「能所一如」的意義，便是沒有自他的分別，沒有物我的分別。一切事，一切處，一切時，一切物，都沒有我；也可以說是一切都是我。只要沒有分別，沒有對待。說是無我也可以，說是唯我也可以。任何事物，都熔化在自我一體以內；而自我也熔化在一切事物以內。是絕對待的自我，而非有對待的自我。這個景象，便是中庸所說的：「合內外之道」；孟子所說的：「上下與天地同流」；老子所說的：「玄同」；莊子所說的：「天地與我並生，萬物與我為一」；王陽明所說的：「天人合一」。黃檗禪師云：「心若平等，不分高下，即與衆生諸佛，世界山河，有相無相，偏十方界，一切平等，無彼我相。此本源清淨心，常自圓滿，光明徧照也」。到達能所一如的境界，只有證悟者才能够有此胸襟。所以僧肇云：「會萬物為自己者，其唯聖人乎」。石頭讀到這兩句時

SO DAPO REMAINED IN THE TEMPLE AND MEDITATED, IMAGINING THAT HE WAS A GIANT WAVE. AT FIRST, HE HAD DIFFICULTY CONCENTRATING, BUT AFTER A WHILE....
!
WAVES BEGAN ROLLING IN....
AND AS THE NIGHT WENT ON, THE WAVES BECAME LARGER AND LARGER, UNTIL THEY KNOCKED OVER VASES AND CARRIED AWAY ITEMS OF WORSHIP...

，嘆賞不已。自己又寫下幾句，以廣其意：「聖人無已，靡所不已，法身無象，誰云自他。圓鑒靈照於其間，萬物體玄而自現。境智非二，孰云去來，至哉斯語也」。佛家特別強調我空、法空、我空之中就無自他的分別；法空之中就無物我的分別。自他、物我的分別都無，即是超越主客。（引自周中一「禪話」）

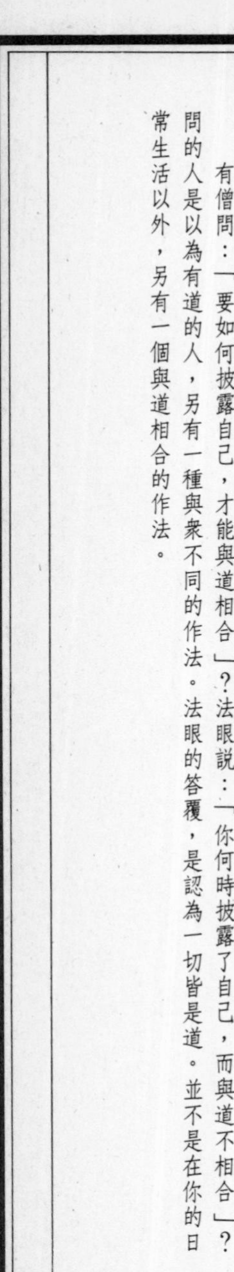

有僧問：「要如何披露自己，才能與道相合」？法眼說：「你何時披露了自己，而與道不相合」？

問的人是以為有道的人，另有一種與衆不同的作法。法眼的答覆，是認為一切皆是道。並不是在你的日常生活以外，另有一個與道相合的作法。

BECAUSE I'M HERE

AN OLD MONK WAS DRYING VEGETABLES UNDER THE SCORCHING SUN....

HOW OLD ARE YOU?

SIXTY-EIGHT.

WHY ARE YOU STILL WORKING SO HARD HERE?

BECAUSE I'M HERE.

BUT WHY ARE YOU WORKING UNDER THE HOT SUN?

BECAUSE THE SUN IS THERE.

!

HEAVEN AND EARTH NURTURE ALL THINGS, BUT WE SHOULD ACT WITHOUT COUNTING ON THE RESULTS AND STRIVE FOR SUCCESS WITHOUT DWELLING ON IT. IF WE JUST WORK HARD WITHOUT COMPLAINING, WE CAN BECOME ONE WITH HEAVEN AND EARTH.

鎌倉壽福寺的益中和尚是繪畫名家，有一天，延光入道到寺拜訪，取出一軸，上書「直指人心，見性成佛」八字，要和尚畫出這種境界之下的「心」。和尚立刻拿起筆來，往他臉上一點，入道非常生氣，和尚就把那副生氣的臉孔畫了出來。入道再要求畫「見性的性」，和尚却拿著筆不畫，只說「畫好了」，入道不了解什麼意思，和尚又說：「你若沒有見性的眼睛就看不到」，入道是個無眼字（未能展開了悟之智眼的人），硬要和尚畫「性」，和尚只好說：「你先拿出性，來讓我瞧瞧，我就替你畫。」，這時入道才無言以對。（「一日一禪」引自「虛堂錄」）

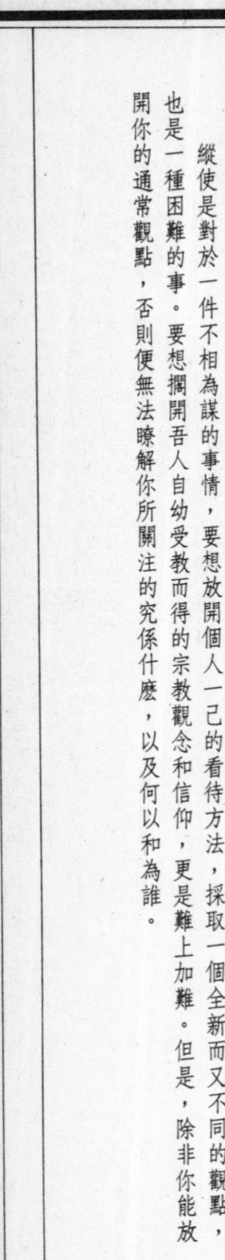

縱使是對於一件不相為謀的事情，要想放開個人一己的看待方法，採取一個全新而又不同的觀點，也是一種困難的事。要想擱開吾人自幼受教而得的宗教觀念和信仰，更是難上加難。但是，除非你能放開你的通常觀點，否則便無法瞭解你所關注的究係什麼，以及何以和為誰。

THE WEEPING LADY

THERE WAS ONCE AN OLD WOMAN KNOWN AS THE "WEEPING LADY" BECAUSE SHE CRIED ALL THE TIME.

ON RAINY DAYS SHE WOULD CRY, AND ON CLEAR DAYS SHE WOULD CRY....

OLD LADY, WHY ARE YOU CRYING ALL THE TIME?

BECAUSE I HAVE TWO DAUGHTERS-- ONE WHO MARRIED A SHOE SALESMAN AND ONE WHO MARRIED AN UMBRELLA SALESMAN.

ON DAYS WHEN THE WEATHER IS GOOD, I THINK OF HOW MY DAUGHTER'S UMBRELLA BUSINESS IS BAD.

AND ON RAINY DAYS, I THINK OF HOW NO ONE WILL GO OUT TO BUY SHOES FROM MY OTHER DAUGHTER!

BUT ON CLEAR DAYS, YOU SHOULD THINK OF HOW GOOD YOUR DAUGHTER'S SHOE BUSINESS IS; AND ON RAINY DAYS, YOU SHOULD THINK OF HOW GOOD YOUR OTHER DAUGHTER'S UMBRELLA BUSINESS IS!

HEY, YOU'RE RIGHT!

FROM THAT DAY ON, THE WEEPING LADY WEPT NO MORE. INSTEAD, SHE CHUCKLED TO HERSELF EVERY DAY REGARDLESS OF THE WEATHER.

IF "THE MIND IS THE BUDDHA," THEN WHETHER A SITUATION IS GOOD OR BAD, ALL DEPENDS ON HOW YOU LOOK AT THE SITUATION.

莊子謂：「至人之用心若鏡，不將不迎，應物而不藏」。後天的知見、完全是經驗的與料，禪師們是不需要這些知見，而是要超越一切知見的。同時禪是無任何對象可以凝思，也不是一種抽象的冥想。他要超越一切知見，才能觸及人的內奥，使你得到一種真、善、美的感覺。經云：「有見即為垢，此則未為見；遠離於諸見，如是乃見佛」。

朱子云：「動時靜便在這裡，動時也有靜。應理而動，則雖動亦靜也。事物之來，若不順理而應，則雖塊然不交於物以求靜，心亦必不得靜。……動靜無端，亦無截然為動為靜之理」。

有沙彌自幼被寺僧收養，從未見過女人。寺僧經常指着仕女畫像告訴沙彌，說是吃人的老虎。沙彌年稍長，隨僧至村市中一行。回寺以後，僧問沙彌云：「你下山所見到的東西，你喜歡那一樣」？沙彌毫不猶疑的說：「我最喜歡吃人的老虎」。食色性也。乃無始以來的習染，斷之最難。多少學道的人，斷送在色字上，所以禪門中有飲酒食肉的禪師，但從不聞犯色戒而能證道者。這是禪人最緊要的一關。

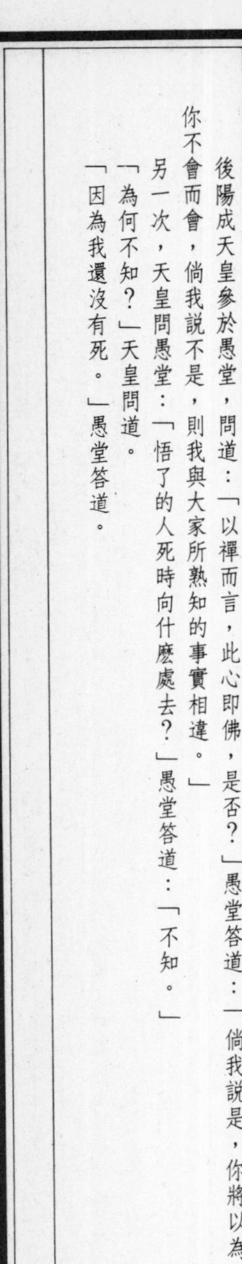
後陽成天皇參於愚堂，問道：「以禪而言，此心即佛，是否？」愚堂答道：「倘我説是，你將以為你不會而會，倘我説不是，則我與大家所熟知的事實相違。」

另一次，天皇問愚堂：「悟了的人死時向什麼處去？」愚堂答道：「不知。」

「為何不知？」天皇問道。

「因為我還沒有死。」愚堂答道。

WHERE DO WE GO AFTER DEATH?

ACCORDING TO ZEN, THIS MIND IS THE BUDDHA, RIGHT?

IF I SAY YES, YOU'LL THINK YOU KNOW WITHOUT REALLY KNOWING, AND IF I SAY NO, I'LL BE DENYING WHAT EVERYONE KNOWS TO BE TRUE.

WHERE DO ENLIGHTENED PEOPLE GO AFTER THEY DIE?

I DON'T KNOW.

WHY DON'T YOU KNOW?

BECAUSE I'M NOT DEAD YET.

WHILE WE LIVE, WE SHOULD ENJOY THE MYSTERY AND BEAUTY THAT ARE LIFE, RATHER THAN WORRYING ABOUT WHAT COMES AFTER DEATH. LIVE TODAY WITHOUT WORRYING ABOUT TOMORROW, FOR TOMORROW WILL HAVE ITS OWN WORRIES.

當此同一境性一旦達到之時，身為劍手的我，也就沒有面對着我並威脅着要刺殺我的對手可見了。我似乎已使我自己變成了對手，而他所做的每一個動作和他所想的每一個念頭，也就是我自己的動作和念頭一樣被我感到了，而我也就直覺地，甚或不知不覺地知道何時以及如何去刺他了。所有這一切，似乎均皆自然而然，毫不勉強。（引自高野武義「劍術心理學」）

禪家有一句流行的口號：「放下屠刀，立地成佛」。屠刀是指習染而言。只要斷除習染，馬上就成佛。無始以來的習心活動，想一下就停下來，這是不可能的事。所以禪家告訴人要想認識自性，必須大死一番。便是以前的我，譬如昨日死，以後的我，譬如今日生。儘管頓悟可以成佛。但在未悟以前，還是經過一番困苦來的。

WITH A SLIGHT FANNING, THE FIRE RETURNS
ONE DAY WHEN THE ZEN MASTER DAHUI ZONGGAO WAS IN THE MOUNTAINS MEDITATING, A RETIRED GENERAL APPROACHED AND INFORMED DAHUI OF HIS INTENT TO BECOME A MONK....
AS SOON AS I ELIMINATE MY BAD HABITS, I'LL RETURN TO BECOME YOUR DISCIPLE.
FINE.
MASTER, I'M READY NOW. I'VE RID MYSELF OF ALL MY BAD HABITS.
WHY DID YOU GET UP SO EARLY? YOUR WIFE IS HOME SLEEPING WITH ANOTHER MAN.
YOU BALD-HEADED MORON! HOW DARE YOU...?!
!
I THINK IT'S A LITTLE EARLY FOR YOU TO BECOME A MONK. YOU'D BETTER RUN ALONG HOME AND PRACTICE MORE SELF-CONTROL.
WORDS AND ACTIONS ARE TWO EXTERIOR MANIFESTATIONS OF OUR INNER THOUGHTS; BUT MOST PEOPLE'S WORDS EXCEED THEIR ACTIONS.

五祖法演禪師云：「我這裡禪如人作賊，引子入人宅，教其子入櫃取衣。子纔入櫃，爺便閉却；並於廳上扣打，驚動主人。自己先逃歸。主人知有賊，點火燭之。賊子在櫃中作鼠嚙聲。主人遣婢開櫃。賊子聳身吹滅燈，推婢走出。主人及家人趕至中路，賊子忽見一井，推巨石投井中，主人於井中覓賊。而賊已逃歸。其父聞知其脫險情形，說你可以做賊了。」禪是要自悟的，在自己的心中，找尋出路，別人幫不了忙的。

有人挖地挖到了尊金羅漢，價值連城，那人却反而十分苦惱，家人問他原因，便回答說：「還有其他十七尊不知埋在那裏呢？」（引自「不亦快哉・中國式幽默笑話」）

日置默仙住在丹波的一座寺院裏。他的一位信徒跑來向他訴苦說他的老婆太吝嗇了。一天，默仙去看這位信徒的太太，在她面前握起一隻拳來。「你是什麼意思？」這位太太訝異地問道。「假如我的拳頭永遠這樣，始終不變，你稱那叫什麼？」他問。「畸形。」這位太太答道。

接着，他又在她眼前把手伸開問道：「假如這隻手永遠這樣，始終不變，你又稱它做什麼？」「還不是畸形？」「只要你多多瞭解這點，」默仙說道，「你就是一位賢內助。」

自此之後，這位太太相夫教子，非常賢慧；不僅節儉，也懂施捨了。

人類生活方式愈趨複雜，所接觸的事物愈多。語言文字。也隨着逐漸增加。衆生成年累月，就被這許許多多代表事物名相的聲音和符號牽着走。東西南北，上下古今，裝滿了一腦子的名相，替人類帶來不少的煩惱，也難怪孔老先生說：「我欲無言」。其實言語所能表詮的一切事物，都是虛花不實。他在自性上是混然一體的，無任何差別之相。千變萬化的波瀾，只有濕性是不變的和相同的。自性亦復如是。在絕對待的自性上，一切名言都安立不上，也就無法用語言來表詮他。所以佛家把一切名言，都稱為增語。假如對自性上加一句增語，便是從識心上所流露出來的。禪師們在證悟以後，絕不肯用語言去表

詮自性。他們教導學人，都是用旁敲側擊的方法。也不直接指出怎樣是自性，同時也不許你說出自性是怎樣的。釋尊在靈山會上，拿着一花朵，面對大衆，不發一語。這時聽衆們都面面相覷，不知所以。只有迦葉尊者會心的一笑。釋尊便高興的說：「我有正法眼藏，涅槃妙心，實相無相，微妙法門，不立文字，教外別傳，付囑摩訶迦葉」。禪就是這樣在不開口的作法中誕生的。

師一夜登山經行，忽雲開見月，大笑一聲，應澧陽東九十許里，居民盡謂東家。明晨迭相推問，直至藥山徒衆云：「昨夜和尚山頂大笑。」李翶再贈詩曰：選得幽居愜野情，終年無送亦無迎；有時直上孤峯頂，月下披雲笑一聲。

其院主僧再三請和尚為人説法，和尚一、二度不許，第三度方始得許。院主便歡喜，先報大衆，大衆喜不自勝，打鐘上來。僧衆纔集，和尚開却門便歸丈室。院主在外責曰：「和尚適來許某甲為人，如今因什摩却不為人，賺某甲？」師曰：「經師自有經師在，論師自有論師在，律師自有律師在，院主恠貧道什摩處？」從此後，從容得數日後，昇座便有人問：「未審和尚承嗣什摩人？」師曰：「古佛殿裏拾得一行字。」進曰：「一行字道什摩？」師曰：「渠不似我，我不似渠」，所以肯這個字。」

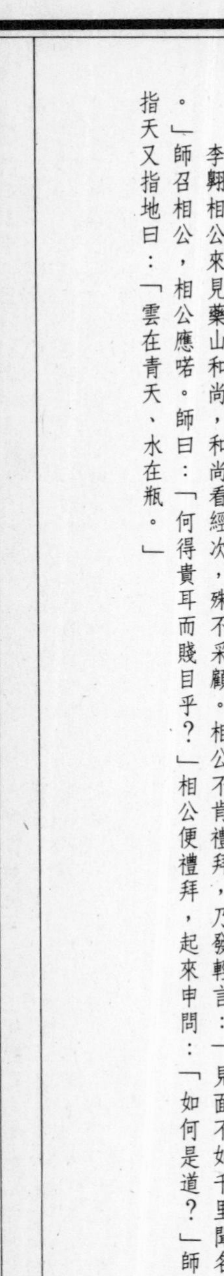
李翱相公來見藥山和尚，和尚看經次，殊不采顧。相公不肯禮拜，乃發輕言：「見面不如千里聞名。」師召相公，相公應喏。師曰：「何得貴耳而賤目乎？」相公便禮拜，起來申問：「如何是道？」師指天又指地曰：「雲在青天、水在瓶。」

CLOUDS IN THE BLUE SKY, WATER IN A BOTTLE

THE FAMOUS SCHOLAR LI AO ONCE PAID A VISIT TO YAOSHAN, BUT AT THE TIME, YAOSHAN WAS BUSY RECITING SCRIPTURES AND SO PAID NO HEED TO HIS VISITOR....

HMPH. HEARING ABOUT HIM WAS ACTUALLY MORE INTERESTING THAN SEEING HIM.

MR. LI !

!

YOU BELIEVE YOUR EARS BUT UNDERESTIMATE YOUR EYES.

PLEASE FORGIVE MY IMPERTINENCE.

MASTER, WHAT IS THE DAO ?

CLOUDS IN THE BLUE SKY AND WATER IN A BOTTLE.

!

DON'T WORRY ABOUT WHETHER THE CLOUDS ARE GOING TO TURN INTO WATER OR WHETHER THE WATER IS GOING TO TURN INTO CLOUDS. IF IT'S CLOUDS, TAKE A CLOUD'S LEISURELY POINT OF VIEW, AND IF IT'S WATER, TAKE WATER'S PLACID, CAREFREE POINT OF VIEW.

SNOWFLAKES FALL WHERE THEY SHOULD
A LAY BUDDHIST BY THE NAME OF PANG ONCE PAID A VISIT TO YAOSHAN. AS HE WAS ABOUT TO LEAVE, YAOSHAN ASKED TWO OF THE MONASTERY'S GUESTS TO SHOW HIM OUT.
PLEASE SHOW HIM OUT.
CERTAINLY.
!
AH, LOOK AT THE GOOD SNOWFLAKES, EACH FALLING IN ITS RIGHTFUL PLACE.
AND WHERE MIGHT THAT BE?
LOOK AT YOU! YOUR EYES SEE LIKE A BLIND MAN AND YOUR MOUTH SPEAKS LIKE A MUTE! YOU CALL YOURSELF A STUDENT OF ZEN?
EVERYTHING UNDER HEAVEN, WHETHER IT BE LARGE OR SMALL, IMPORTANT OR INSIGNIFICANT, HAS ITS OWN PARTICULAR PLACE. AND WHEN IT ARRIVES IN ITS RIGHTFUL PLACE, WHY ASK WHY? THAT'S JUST HOW IT IS!

舉龐居士辭藥山，山命十人禪客相送，至門首，居士指空中雪，云：「好雪片片，不落別處。」時有全禪客云：「落在什麼處？」士打一掌，全云：「居士也不得草草。」士云：「汝恁麼稱禪客？閻老子未放汝在。」全云：「居士作麼生？」士又打一掌，云：「眼見如盲，口說如啞。」

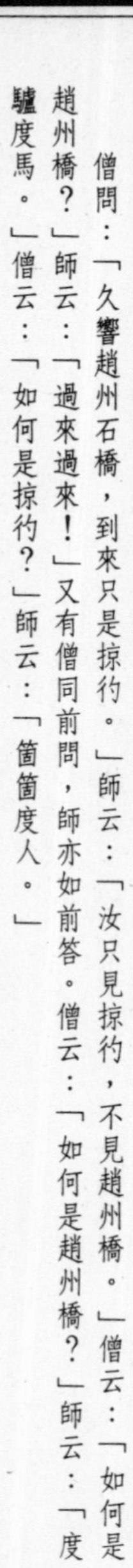
僧問：「久響趙州石橋，到來只是掠彴。」師云：「汝只見掠彴，不見趙州橋。」僧云：「如何是趙州橋？」師云：「過來過來！」又有僧同前問，師亦如前答。僧云：「如何是趙州橋？」師云：「度驢度馬。」僧云：「如何是掠彴？」師云：「箇箇度人。」

ZHAOZHOU'S STONE BRIDGE

IT HAS BEEN SAID THAT NEAR THE GUANYIN MONASTERY IN HEBEI PROVINCE, THERE WAS A FAMOUS BRIDGE CALLED THE ZHAOZHOU (CHAO-CHOU) STONE BRIDGE....

I HAVE HEARD SAY OF THE ZHAOZHOU STONE BRIDGE, BUT WHEN I ARRIVED, ALL I SAW WAS A BRIDGE MADE OUT OF A SINGLE LOG. WHERE'S THE STONE BRIDGE?

YOU SAW ONLY THE SINGLE LOG, AND YOU DIDN'T SEE THE STONE BRIDGE.

THAT'S RIGHT. WHAT EXACTLY IS ZHAOZHOU'S STONE BRIDGE?

IT IS THE BRIDGE THAT ALLOWS THE CROSSING OF DONKEYS, HORSES, AND EVERY CONFUSED BEING IN THE WORLD.

THE ACTUAL SINGLE LOG BRIDGE COULD LET ONLY ONE PERSON CROSS AT A TIME, BUT THROUGH THE MERCY OF ZHAOZHOU, HIS ABSTRACT STONE BRIDGE ALLOWED ALL BEINGS TO QUIETLY CROSS AT THE SAME TIME.

僧問：「學人迷昧，乞師指示」。師云：「喫粥也未」？僧云：「喫粥也」。師云：「洗鉢去」。
其僧忽然省悟。

夫求法者，應無所求。心外無別佛，佛外無別心。不取善，不捨惡，淨穢兩邊，俱不依怙。達罪性空，念念不可得，無自性故。三界唯心，森羅萬象，一法之所印。……若體此意，但可隨時著衣吃飯，長養聖胎，任運過時，更有何事。（馬祖語）

◉著衣吃飯即表示平常的生活。將平常生活原原本本絲毫不加作為，而任運無作地活下去，就是馬祖的禪的生活方式。如果是一般人，則必須加以作為、扭曲才能活下去，亦即平時不斷在生活上激起波瀾，而這就是現實的生活方式。若要虛心而悠悠自適的生活，就必須無心。

問：一栢樹子還有佛性也無」？師曰：「有」。曰：「幾時成佛」？師曰：「待虛空落地時」。曰：「幾時虛空落地」？師曰：「待栢樹子成佛時」。

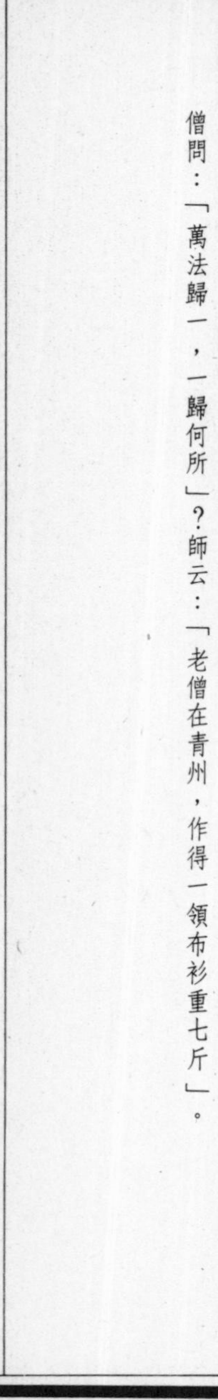
僧問：「萬法歸一，一歸何所」？師云：「老僧在青州，作得一領布衫重七斤」。

THE MANY RETURN TO ONE
ALL THINGS RETURN TO ONE, BUT WHERE DOES THE ONE RETURN TO ?
WHEN I WAS IN QINGZHOU, I MADE A ROBE THAT WEIGHED SEVEN POUNDS.

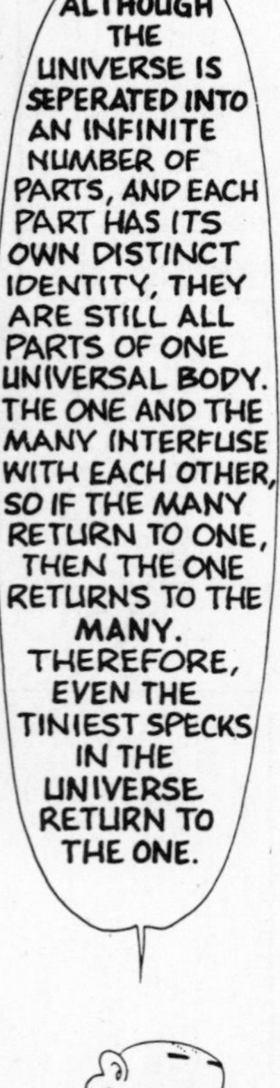
ALTHOUGH THE UNIVERSE IS SEPERATED INTO AN INFINITE NUMBER OF PARTS, AND EACH PART HAS ITS OWN DISTINCT IDENTITY, THEY ARE STILL ALL PARTS OF ONE UNIVERSAL BODY. THE ONE AND THE MANY INTERFUSE WITH EACH OTHER, SO IF THE MANY RETURN TO ONE, THEN THE ONE RETURNS TO THE MANY. THEREFORE, EVEN THE TINIEST SPECKS IN THE UNIVERSE RETURN TO THE ONE.

僧問趙州：「如何是趙州？」州云：「東門、西門、南門、北門。」

有僧遊五臺，問一婆子：「臺山路向什麼處去」？婆子云：「驀直恁麼去」。僧便去，婆子云：「又恁麼去也」。其僧舉似師。師云：「待我去勘破遮婆子」。師至明日，便去問：「臺山路向什麼處去」？婆子云：「驀直恁麼去」。師便去。婆子云：「又恁麼去也」。師歸院謂僧曰：「我為汝勘破婆子了也」。

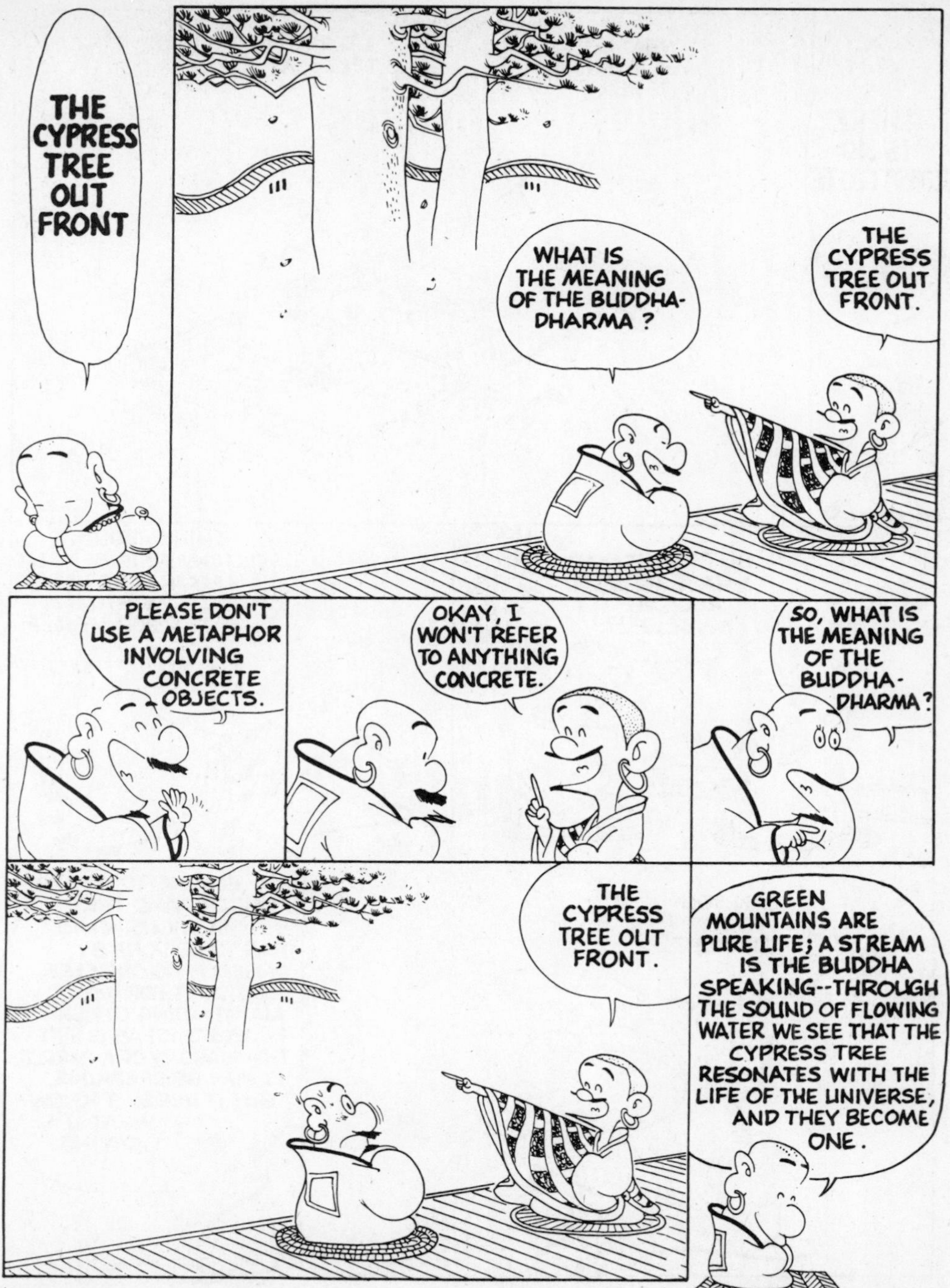

問：「如何是祖師西來意」？師曰：「庭前栢樹子」。曰：「和尚莫將境示人」。師曰：「我不將境示人」。曰：「如何是祖師西來意」？師曰：「庭前栢樹子」。

宗教的體驗，是以自己來明白自己的，是自身獨自得到的絶對境。

趙州和尚六十歲開始學禪，直到八十歲仍在到處參學，那時他已大悟了。他從八十歲開始教學，直到一百二十歲逝世為止。一個學生問他：「一物不將來時如何？」趙州答云：「放下着！」「一物也無，教我放下個什麼？」「放不下就提取去！」問者於此有省（「禪話一〇一則」引）

◉「將來」含有「拿來」、「帶來」之意。

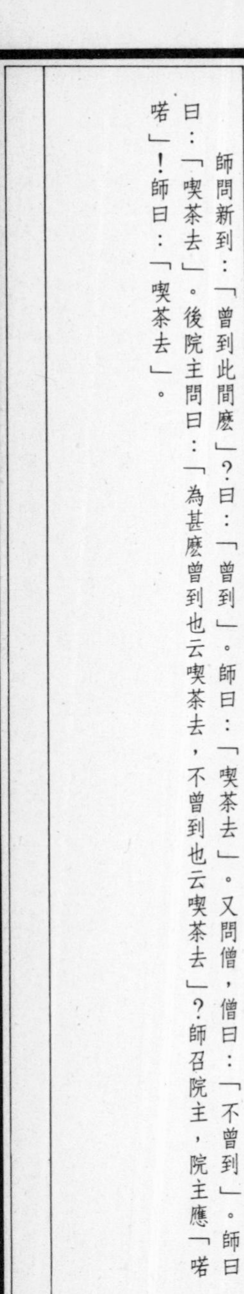

師問新到：「曾到此間麼」？曰：「曾到」。師曰：「喫茶去」。又問僧，僧曰：「不曾到」。師曰曰：「喫茶去」。後院主問曰：「為甚麼曾到也云喫茶去，不曾到也云喫茶去」？師召院主，院主應「喏喏」！師曰：「喫茶去」。

HAVE SOME TEA

HAVE YOU BEEN HERE BEFORE?

YES, I HAVE.

GO IN AND HAVE SOME TEA.

YES, SIR.

HAVE YOU BEEN HERE BEFORE?

THIS IS MY FIRST TIME HERE.

GO IN AND HAVE SOME TEA.

!

YES, SIR.

WHAT'S THAT SUPPOSED TO MEAN? THEY GET TEA IF THEY'VE COME BEFORE, AND THEY GET TEA IF THEY HAVEN'T.

PROCTOR!

GO IN AND HAVE SOME TEA.

WHETHER THEY HAD BEEN THERE BEFORE OR NOT, ZHAOZHOU DID NOT DIFFERENTIATE AND INVITED THEM ALL TO TEA. ALTHOUGH A CUP OF TEA IS JUST AN EXPRESSION OF THE ORDINARY MIND, IT IS THE KEY TO ZEN.

A NATIVE OF JIANNAN IN SICHUAN, XUANJIAN'S (HSÜAN-CHIEN) ORIGINAL SURNAME WAS ZHOU. HE LEFT HOME TO JOIN THE MONKHOOD AT AN EARLY AGE AND EXTENSIVELY STUDIED THE DOCTRINES OF DISCIPLINE. HE LEARNED THE ENTIRE *DIAMOND SŪTRA* BY HEART, AND BECAUSE OF THIS HE BECAME KNOWN AS DIAMOND ZHOU.

LATER, HE LEARNED THAT THE RIVAL SOUTHERN SCHOOL OF ZEN HAD GAINED A GREAT FOLLOWING. INFLAMED BY THIS, HE HEADED SOUTH TO CHALLENGE THEIR TEACHINGS. HIS MONASTERY WAS LATER LOCATED AT DESHAN (TE-SHAN) IN HUNAN PROVINCE, SO PEOPLE REFER TO HIM AS DESHAN.

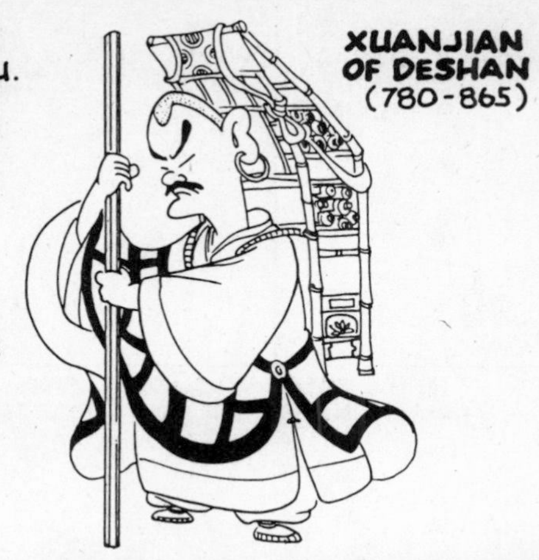

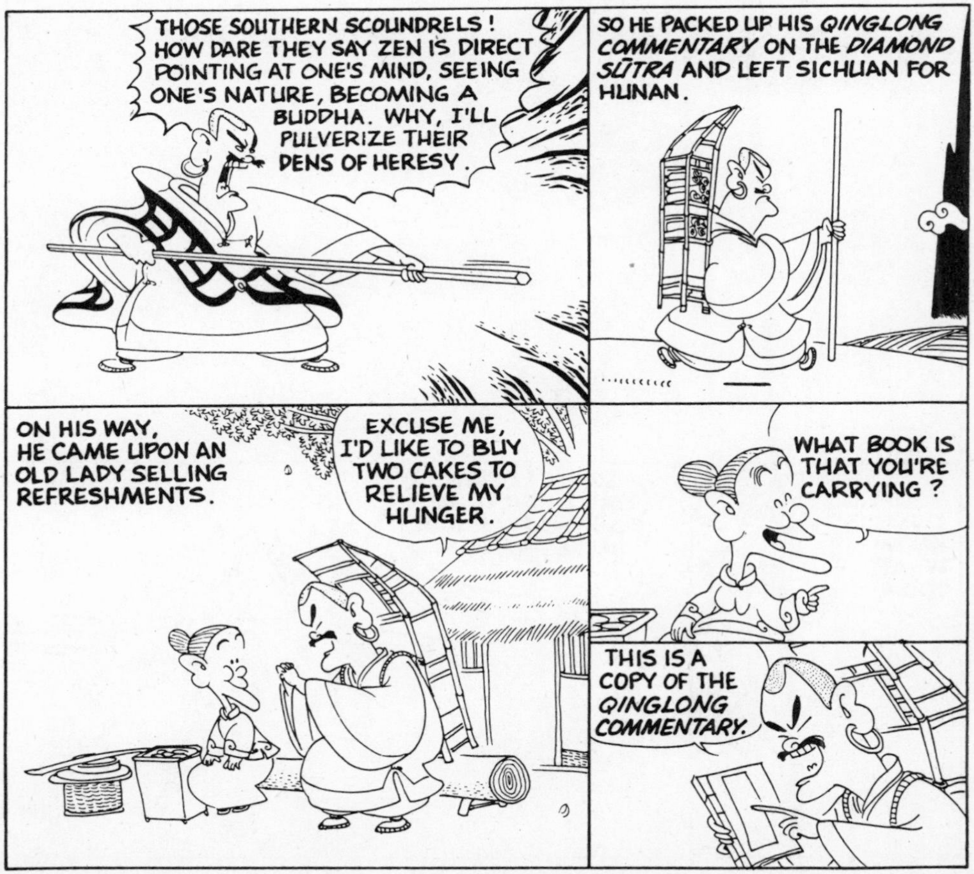

XUANJIAN OF DESHAN (780-865)

THOSE SOUTHERN SCOUNDRELS! HOW DARE THEY SAY ZEN IS DIRECT POINTING AT ONE'S MIND, SEEING ONE'S NATURE, BECOMING A BUDDHA. WHY, I'LL PULVERIZE THEIR DENS OF HERESY.

SO HE PACKED UP HIS *QINGLONG COMMENTARY* ON THE *DIAMOND SŪTRA* AND LEFT SICHUAN FOR HUNAN.

ON HIS WAY, HE CAME UPON AN OLD LADY SELLING REFRESHMENTS.

EXCUSE ME, I'D LIKE TO BUY TWO CAKES TO RELIEVE MY HUNGER.

WHAT BOOK IS THAT YOU'RE CARRYING?

THIS IS A COPY OF THE *QINGLONG COMMENTARY.*

龍潭因德山請益，抵夜，潭云：「夜深，子何不下去？」山遂珍重揭簾而出，見外面黑，却回云：「外面黑！」潭乃點紙燭度與。山擬接，潭便吹滅。山於此忽然有省，便作禮。潭云：「子見個甚麼道理？」山云：「某甲從今日去不疑天下老和尚舌頭也。」至明日，龍潭陞座云：「可中有個漢，牙如劍樹，口似血盆，一棒打不回頭；他時異日，向孤峯頂上立吾道去在！」山遂取疏抄，於法堂前將一炬火提起云：「窮諸玄辯，若一毫致於太虛；竭世樞機，似一滴投於巨壑！」將疏抄便燒，於是禮辭。

無門曰：德山未出關時，心憤憤，口悱悱，得得來南方，要滅却教外別傳之旨。及到澧州路上，問婆子買點心。婆云：「大德，車子內是什麼文字？」山云：「金剛經疏抄。」婆云：「只如經中道：過去心不可得，現在心不可得，未來心不可得。大德要點哪個心？」德山被者一問，直得口似扁擔。然雖如是，未肯向婆子句下死却。遂問婆子：「近處有甚宗師？」婆云：「五里外有龍潭和尚。」及到龍潭，納盡敗闕，可謂是前言不應後語！龍潭大似憐兒不覺醜，見他有些子火種時，即忙將惡水驀頭一澆澆殺。

師尋常遇僧到參，多以挂杖打，臨濟聞之，遣侍者來參，教令：「德山若打汝，但接取挂杖，當胸一挂」。侍者到，方禮拜，師乃打，侍者接得挂杖與一挂，師歸方丈。侍者迴舉似臨濟，濟云：「從來疑遮個漢」。師上堂曰：「問即有過，不問又乖」。有僧出禮拜，師便打，僧曰：「某甲始禮拜，為什麼便打」？師曰：「待汝開口堪作什麼」！師令侍者喚義存，（雪峰）存上來，師曰：「我自喚存，汝又來什麼」？存無對。師因疾，有僧問：「還有不病者無」？師曰：「有」。問：「如何是不病者」？師曰：「阿爺阿爺」。

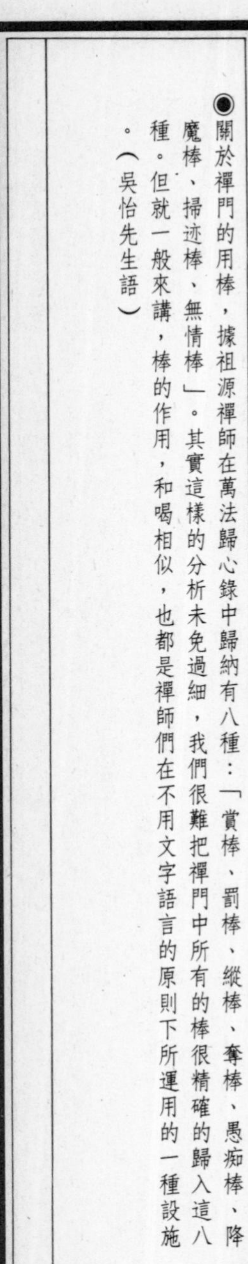
◉關於禪門的用棒，據祖源禪師在萬法歸心錄中歸納有八種：「賞棒、罰棒、縱棒、奪棒、愚痴棒、降魔棒、掃迹棒、無情棒」。其實這樣的分析未免過細，我們很難把禪門中所有的棒很精確的歸入這八種。但就一般來講，棒的作用，和喝相似，也都是禪師們在不用文字語言的原則下所運用的一種設施。（吴怡先生語）

LONGTAN SUDDENLY BLEW OUT THE CANDLE, AND IT WAS AT THIS TIME THAT DESHAN ATTAINED ENLIGHTENMENT.

THE NEXT DAY, DESHAN TOOK HIS COPY OF THE *QINGLONG COMMENTARY* TO THE MAIN HALL AND BURNED IT RIGHT THERE.

LEARNING ALL THE VARIOUS PROFOUND PHILOSOPHIES IS LIKE A MERE STRAND OF HAIR IN THE VASTNESS OF SPACE; COMPLETELY UNDERSTANDING THE FUNDAMENTAL FORCES OF THE WORLD IS LIKE A MERE DROP IN A GIANT ABYSS.

IT IS NOT UNTIL THE EXTERNAL LIGHT IS EXTINGUISHED THAT OUR INTERNAL LIGHT SHINES BRIGHT. IT IS NOT UNTIL OUR CRUTCH IS DISCARDED THAT WE CAN REALIZE OUR LATENT POTENTIAL.

YIXUAN OF LINJI, FOUNDER OF THE LINJI (RINZAI) SCHOOL (?-867)

LINJI YIXUAN (LIN-CHI I-HSÜAN) WAS A NATIVE OF CAO COUNTY IN SHANDONG PROVINCE AND HIS LAY SURNAME WAS XING. WHILE STILL A CHILD, HE DECIDED TO LEAVE HIS FAMILY TO BECOME A MONK, AND HE PURSUED THE TRUTH WITH GREAT SINCERITY. AROUND THE AGE OF TWENTY, HE WENT TO ANHUI PROVINCE AND STUDIED UNDER HUANGBO. AFTER ATTAINING ENLIGHTENMENT, HE SETTLED DOWN IN ZHENZHOU, HEBEI PROVINCE, AND ESTABLISHED THE LINJI MONASTERY, WHERE HE PREACHED HIS OWN STYLE OF ZEN.

THE STAFF!
LINJI OFTEN USED THE SHOUT TO INDUCE ENLIGHTENMENT IN HIS STUDENTS, AND HIS SHOUT BECAME LIKENED TO DESHAN'S USE OF THE STAFF.
THE SHOUT!
A SIDE EFFECT OF THIS PRACTICE WAS THAT LINJI'S STUDENTS KNEW ONLY HOW TO IMITATE HIS USE OF THE SHOUT, BUT KNEW NOTHING OF ITS FUNCTION OR ITS MEANING....
HA
HA

師諱義玄，曹州南華人也，俗姓邢。幼而穎異，及落髮受具，志慕禪宗。師在黃檗三年，行業純一，首座乃嘆曰：「雖是後生，與衆有異。」遂問：「上座在此多少時？」師云：「三年。」首座云：「曾參問也無？」師云：「不曾參問，不知問箇什麽？」首座云：「汝何不去問堂頭和尚，如何是佛法的大意？」師便去問，聲未絶，黃檗便打，師下來，首座云：「問話作麽生？」師云：「某甲問聲未絶，和尚便打，某甲不會。」首座云：「但更去問！」師又去問，黃檗又打，如是三度發問，三度被打。

有一次，臨濟禪師上堂對大家說：「汝等總學我喝，我今問汝有一人從東堂出，一人從西堂出，兩人齊聲一喝，者裏分得賓主麼？汝且作麼生分，若分不得已，後不得學老僧喝。」

臨濟為了防止學人濫用「喝」字，而提出這個公案，主要在於叫人認清主客本是一體，它是無賓無主，就是真正的真我。（事見「指月錄」）

師（臨濟義玄）謂僧曰：「有時一喝如金剛王寶劍，有時一喝如踞地師子，有時一喝如探竿影草，有時一喝不作一喝用。汝作麼生會」。僧擬議，師便喝。（五燈會元）

上堂，有僧出禮拜，師便喝，僧云：「老和尚，莫探頭好！」師云：「你道落在什麼處？」僧便喝。又有僧問：「如何是佛法大意？」師便喝，僧禮拜，師云：「你道好喝也無？」僧云：「草賊大敗。」師云：「過在什麼處？」僧云：「再犯不容。」師云：「大衆要會臨濟賓主句，問取堂中二禪客。」便下座。

師到初祖塔頭，塔主云：「長老先禮佛，先禮祖？」師云：「佛祖俱不禮塔。」主云：「佛祖與長老是什麼寃家？」師便拂袖而出。

◉初祖塔頭：塔是梵文墳墓的音譯。

潭州漸源仲興禪師，在道吾處為典座，一日隨道吾往檀越家弔喪，師以手拊棺曰：「生耶死耶？」道吾曰：「生也不道，死也不道。」師曰：「為什麼不道？」道吾曰：「不道不道！」弔畢同迴，途次，師曰：「和尚今日須與仲興道，儻更不道，即打去也。」道吾曰：「打即任打，生也不道死也不道。」師遂打道吾數拳。道吾歸院，令師且去：「少間主事知了打汝。」師乃禮辭往石霜，舉前語及打道吾之事今請和尚道。石霜曰：「汝不見道吾道：『生也不道死也不道？』」師於此大悟。乃設齋懺悔，師一

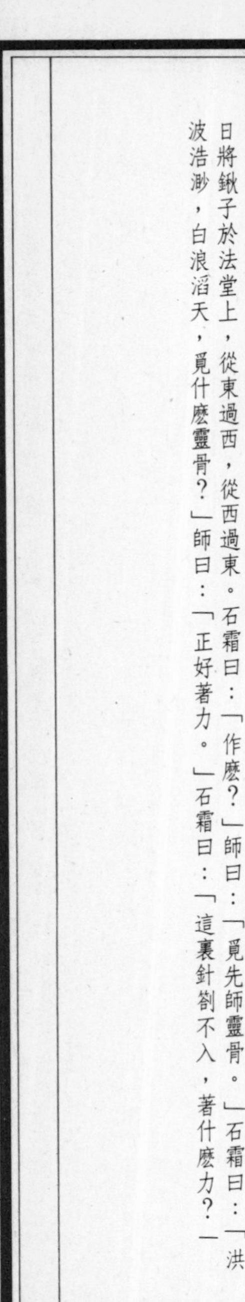
日將鍬子於法堂上，從東過西，從西過東。石霜曰：「作麼？」師曰：「覓先師靈骨。」石霜曰：「洪波浩渺，白浪滔天，覓什麼靈骨？」師曰：「正好著力。」石霜曰：「這裏針劄不入，著什麼力？」

AFTER A TIME, DAOWU PASSED AWAY. JIANYUAN SOUGHT OUT ANOTHER TEACHER NAMED SHISHUANG AND ASKED HIM THE SAME QUESTION.

YOU CAN'T SAY HE'S ALIVE, AND YOU CAN'T SAY HE'S DEAD.

UPON HEARING THIS, JIANYUAN WAS SUDDENLY ENLIGHTENED.

ANOTHER DAY, HE WAS FOUND CARRYING A HOE AND PACING UP AND DOWN THE TEMPLE HALL.

WHAT ARE YOU DOING?

I'M SEARCHING FOR THE MASTER'S RELICS.

FLOODING WATERS REACH FAR AND WIDE; WHITE WAVES INUNDATE THE HEAVENS. WHAT RELICS ARE THERE TO LOOK FOR?

I'M DOING MY BEST.

WHEN WE ARE ALIVE, LIFE IS EVERYTHING TO US. AS FOR DEAD PEOPLE, DEATH IS EVERYTHING TO THEM. WHILE YOU ARE ALIVE, CONCENTRATE ON LIVING. THIS WAY, YOU WON'T BE APPRENSIVE ABOUT DEATH.

婺州金華山俱胝和尚，初住庵，有尼名實際到庵，戴笠子執錫繞師三帀，云：「道得，即拈下笠子。」三問，師皆無對尼便去師曰：「日勢稍晚，且留一宿。」尼曰：「道得，即宿。」師又無對尼去後，歎曰：「我雖處丈夫之形，而無丈夫之氣。」擬棄庵往諸方參尋，其夜山神告曰：「不須離此山，將有大菩薩來為和尚説法也。」果旬日，天龍和尚到庵，師乃迎禮，具陳前事天龍豎一指而示之，師當下大悟。自此凡有參學僧到，師唯舉一指，無別提唱。有一童子於外被人詰曰：「和尚説何法要？」童子

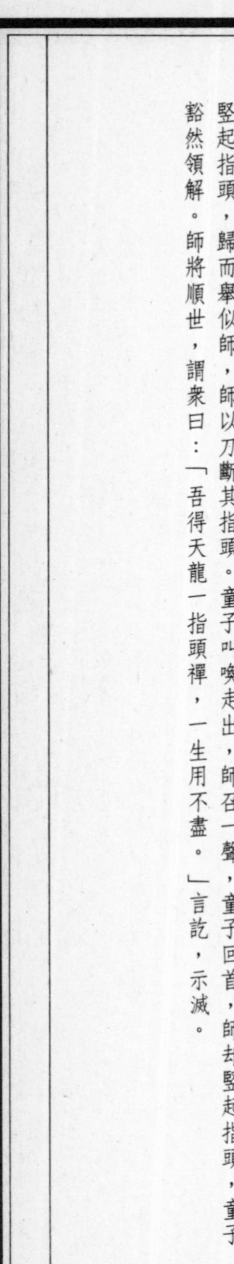

豎起指頭，歸而舉似師，師以刀斷其指頭。童子叫喚走出，師召一聲，童子回首，師却豎起指頭，童子豁然領解。師將順世，謂衆曰：「吾得天龍一指頭禪，一生用不盡。」言訖，示滅。

OH! STUMPED BY A NUN! HOW CAN I STAY HERE AND CALL THIS SELF-CULTIVATION?

SO THAT NIGHT HE PACKED HIS THINGS AND PREPARED TO HEAD DOWN THE MOUNTAIN AT FIRST LIGHT.

ZZZ

YOUNG MONK, YOU APPEAR TROUBLED. WHAT MIGHT BE THE MATTER?

!

AND JUZHI RELATED IN DETAIL THE EVENT OF THE PREVIOUS DAY....

HAVING THE BODY OF A MAN IS USELESS WITHOUT THE DIGNITY OF ONE. I CAN'T ANSWER EVEN A NUN'S QUESTION....

WOULD YOU LIKE TO KNOW THE CORRECT ANSWER?

PLEASE TELL ME, MASTER.

ALL TRUTHS ARE HERE!

用傷害人體的方法以開示佛法，真是一件不可思議的事。假如俱胝沒有使童子因此而得開悟的把握，我想他不會如此荒唐。此種動作，絕不是一般人所能倣法的：由俱胝的因豎指而得悟，童子的因無指而得悟，可以肯定一點。就是禪師接人，不拘某一種形象。他們是因勢利導，具有超越形象的作用。從他們師弟二人開悟的情形分析：俱胝初見尼時，從他自己感歎無丈夫氣一語來說，他是着了男女相。所以對尼的問話，不能道得。天然豎起一指，表示在自性上是平等一如的，本無男女之相。一是絕待的象

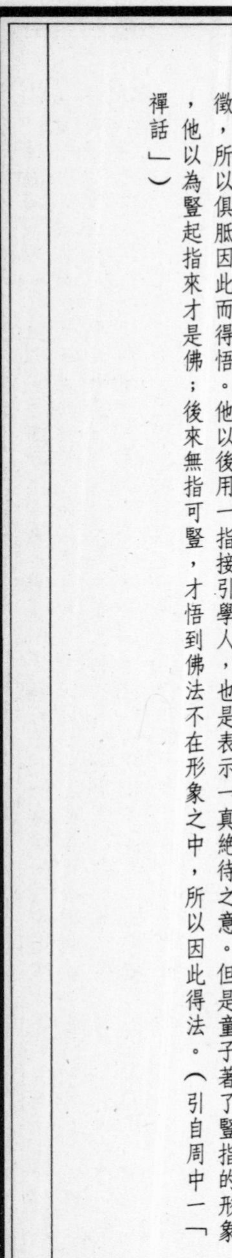

徵，所以俱胝因此而得悟。他以後用一指接引學人，也是表示一真絶待之意。但是童子著了豎指的形象，他以為豎起指來才是佛；後來無指可豎，才悟到佛法不在形象之中，所以因此得法。（引自周中一「禪話」）

BACK IT GOES AGAIN TO BEING A STILL, SILENT SUMMIT TOWERING ABOVE, AND IF YOU RAISE YOUR HEAD, A BREEZE WILL FILL YOUR EARS

....

I UNDERSTAND NOW, MASTER-- THE ONE IS ALL THINGS, AND ALL THINGS ARE THE ONE !

MASTER!... MASTER ? HE'S GONE..

!

FROM THIS TIME FORWARD, WHENEVER THE ZEN MASTER JUZHI WAS ASKED ABOUT THE BUDDHA-DHARMA, HE SIMPLY BROUGHT OUT HIS THUMB AND SAID....

THIS !

!

"THE MANY HAVE ONE ESSENCE, AND THE ONE HAS MANY MANIFESTATIONS." THERE ARE INNUMERABLE DIFFERENCES AMONG THINGS IN THE WORLD, AND YET EVERYTHING ORIGINATES IN ONE SOURCE. "THE WORLD IS A FINGER"; SO THERE IS NO DIFFERENCE BETWEEN A FINGER AND THE MYRIAD THINGS.

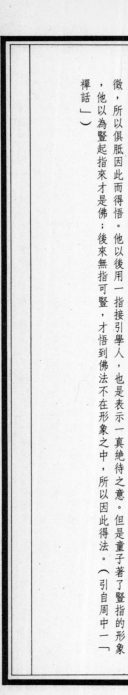

俱胝和尚，凡有詰問，唯舉一指。後有童子，因外人問：「和尚說何法要？」童子亦豎指頭。胝聞，遂以刄斷其指，童子負痛號哭而去。胝復召之，童子廻首，胝却豎起指頭，童子忽然領悟。胝將順世，謂衆曰：「吾得天龍一指頭禪，一生受用不盡！」言訖示滅。

無門曰：俱胝並童子悟處不在指頭上，若向者裏見得，天龍同俱胝並童子與自己一串穿却！頌曰：

俱胝鈍置老天龍，利刄單提勘小童。巨靈擡手無多子，分破華山千萬重！

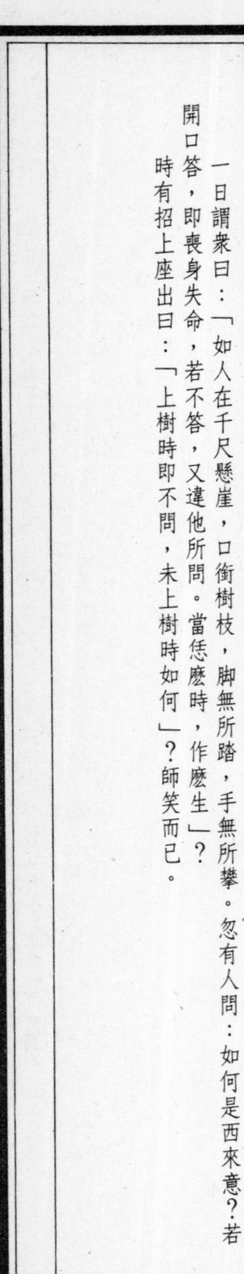

一日謂衆曰：「如人在千尺懸崖，口銜樹枝，脚無所踏，手無所攀。忽有人問：如何是西來意？若開口答，即喪身失命，若不答，又違他所問。當恁麼時，作麼生」？時有招上座出曰：「上樹時即不問，未上樹時如何」？師笑而已。

XIANGYAN UP A TREE

XIANGYAN ZHIXIAN SAID TO HIS DISCIPLES:

THERE WAS ONCE A MAN WHO CLIMBED A TREE AND HUNG THERE BY HIS TEETH. THEN ANOTHER PERSON CAME ALONG AND SAID:

EXCUSE ME, WHAT IS THE MEANING OF THE BUDDHA-DHARMA?

IF THE MAN IN THE TREE DIDN'T RESPOND TO THE QUESTION, HE WOULD BE SHOWING DISRESPECT TO THE QUESTIONER;

AND IF HE DID ANSWER, HE WOULD FALL AND BREAK HIS NECK....

TELL ME, HOW SHOULD HE HAVE ESCAPED THIS PREDICAMENT?

I WON'T ASK WHAT HE SHOULD HAVE DONE IN THE TREE, BUT RATHER, WHAT HE WAS LIKE BEFORE HE CLIMBED THE TREE.

HA-HA-HA.

IN REGARD TO THE FUNDAMENTAL TRUTH, WHICH PRECEDES WORDLESSNESS, LIFE BEFORE WORDLESSNESS SHOULD BE USED IN RESPONSE.

SAME DESTINATION, DIFFERENT PATHS
A STUDENT ONCE ASKED THE MONK BALING:
IS THERE ANY DIFFERENCE BETWEEN WHAT THE PATRIARCHS SAID AND WHAT THE SCRIPTURES SAY ?
WHEN IT GETS COLD, PHEASANTS ROOST IN TREES,
AND DUCKS GO UNDER-WATER.
!
IT'S COLD FOR BOTH, BUT EACH HAS A DIFFERENT WAY OF DEALING WITH IT. EVERYONE HAS A DIFFERENT WAY OF ARRIVING AT THE SAME DESTINATION. THERE IS NOT JUST ONE PATH, AND NOT EVERYONE IS FIT TO TRAVEL THE SAME PATH. BY LIMITING YOURSELF TO A CERTAIN PATH, YOU MAY ACTUALLY LEAD YOURSELF ASTRAY.

僧問：「祖意教意是同是別？」師曰：「雞寒上樹，鴨寒入水。」僧問三乘

善靜在普樂處典園務。有僧辭普樂。普曰：「四面是山，闍黎向什麼處去」？僧無對。語善靜。靜代對曰：「竹密不妨流水過，山高那阻野雲飛」。僧白普樂。普曰：「非汝之言」。僧具言園頭所教。普樂上堂謂衆曰：「莫輕園頭，他日住一城隍，五百人常隨也」。後果如其言。四面是山，指一切障道逆緣而言。此心大無大相，小無小相。但得心無罣碍，隨處可通。僧殆拘於四山之形象，故不能對。

LOOKING BUT NOT SEEING
ONE DAY WHILE THE MONK NANQUAN WAS WORKING IN THE HILLS, A TRAVELLING MONK APPROACHED TO ASK DIRECTIONS:
EXCUSE ME, CAN YOU TELL ME HOW TO GET TO THE FAMOUS NANQUAN MONASTERY?
I PAID THREE DOLLARS FOR THIS SICKLE.
I WASN'T ASKING ABOUT THE SICKLE, I JUST WANT TO KNOW HOW TO GET TO THE MONASTERY.
AND IT'S VERY USEFUL BECAUSE IT'S SO SHARP.
BY EMPHASIZING APPEARANCES, WE MISS THE REAL THING. IN PAYING TOO MUCH ATTENTION TO NAMES AND REPUTATIONS, WE CAN LAY EYES ON WHAT WE'RE LOOKING FOR BUT MISS IT COMPLETELY.

有一天，南泉和尚在山上作務時，有位旅僧經過而問道：
「有名的南泉禪院，不知如何走？」
南泉答道：「我是花了三十錢買了這把鎌刀的。」
僧侶又説：「我並不是問你鎌刀的事，而問你如何到南泉禪院。」
南泉答説：「這把鎌刀使用起來十分鋭利。」（事見「葛藤集」）

唐朝的李勃是一個有名的讀書人，由於讀書破萬卷，人稱之為「李萬卷」。有一次，李勃拜訪廬山業宗寺的智常和尚，問：「在佛典裏，有須彌山沒入罌粟種子之中的説法，但是，這要從何説起呢？」，於是和尚就反問：「人稱你是李萬卷，但是，萬卷書怎樣裝入你這小小的腦袋瓜子裏呢？」，李勃乃豁然大悟。

◉在「維摩經」「不可思議品」中有「須彌入芥子之中」、「以四大海水入一毛孔」的説法。意即世界的中心妙高山繞行可納入一顆罌粟子之中，環繞着這座大山的四方之海亦可沒入一個毛孔裏。

WITHERED TREE ZEN
THERE WAS ONCE AN OLD LADY WHO BUILT A GRASS HUT AND SUPPORTED A MONK'S EFFORTS AT SELF-CULTIVATION FOR TWENTY YEARS.
NAMAḤ AMITĀBHA
AND EVERY DAY A BEAUTIFUL YOUNG WOMAN BROUGHT HIM HIS MEALS.
WHEN YOU SEND HIM HIS FOOD, LET'S TEST HOW HIS SELF-CULTIVATION IS COMING ALONG. GIVE HIM A HUG AND SEE HOW HE REACTS.
OKAY.
HOW DOES THIS FEEL ?
IT FEELS LIKE A WITHERED TREE LEANING AGAINST A WINTRY CLIFF; LIKE A FRIGID WINTER DAY WITHOUT A TRACE OF WARMTH....
TWENTY YEARS WASTED ON A SCOUNDREL !
UPON HEARING WHAT THE MONK HAD SAID, THE OLD LADY WAS INFURIATED AND SET FIRE TO THE MONK'S HUT.
GRANTED, THE MONK SHOULD REFUSE SUCH A TEMPTATION, BUT AFTER TWENTY YEARS OF SELF-CULTIVATION, HE SHOULD ALSO HAVE MORE LOVING KINDNESS AND COMPASSION. HE WAS INDEED A SCOUNDREL.

昔有一婆子，供養一庵主經二十年，常使一二八女子送飯給侍。一日，使子女抱曰：「正恁麼時如何？」主曰：「枯木倚寒岩，三冬無暖氣。」女子舉示婆。婆曰：「我二十年，只供養一個俗漢。」終於遣出燒庵。

瑞巖師彥和尚，每日自喚：「主人公！」復自應：「諾！」乃云：「惺惺着！」「喏！」「他時異日莫受人瞞！」「喏！喏！」

無門曰：瑞巖老子自買自賣，弄出許多神頭鬼面。何故聻？一個喚底，一個應底；一個惺惺底，一個不受人瞞底。認着依前還不是！若也傚他，總是野狐見解！頌曰：學道之人不識真，只為從前認識神。無量劫來生死本，癡人喚作本來人！

◉惺惺着：警惕語，清醒些之意！

元和中（八〇六—八一九年），白居易出守茲郡，因入山禮謁，乃問師曰：「禪師住處甚危險」。師曰：「太守危險尤甚」。曰：「弟子位鎮江山，何險之有」？師曰：「薪火相交，識性不停，得非險乎」？

又問：「如何是佛法大意」？師曰：「諸惡莫作，衆善奉行」。白曰：「三歲孩兒也解恁麼道」。師曰：「三歲孩兒雖道得，八十老人行不得」。白遂作禮。

有源律師來問：「和尚修道，還用功否」？師曰：「用功」。曰：「如何用功」？師曰：「饑來喫飯，困來眠」。曰：「一切人總如同師用功否」？師曰：「不同」。曰：「何故不同」？師曰：「他喫飯時不肯喫飯，百種須索；睡時不肯睡，千般計校，所以不同也」。律師杜口。

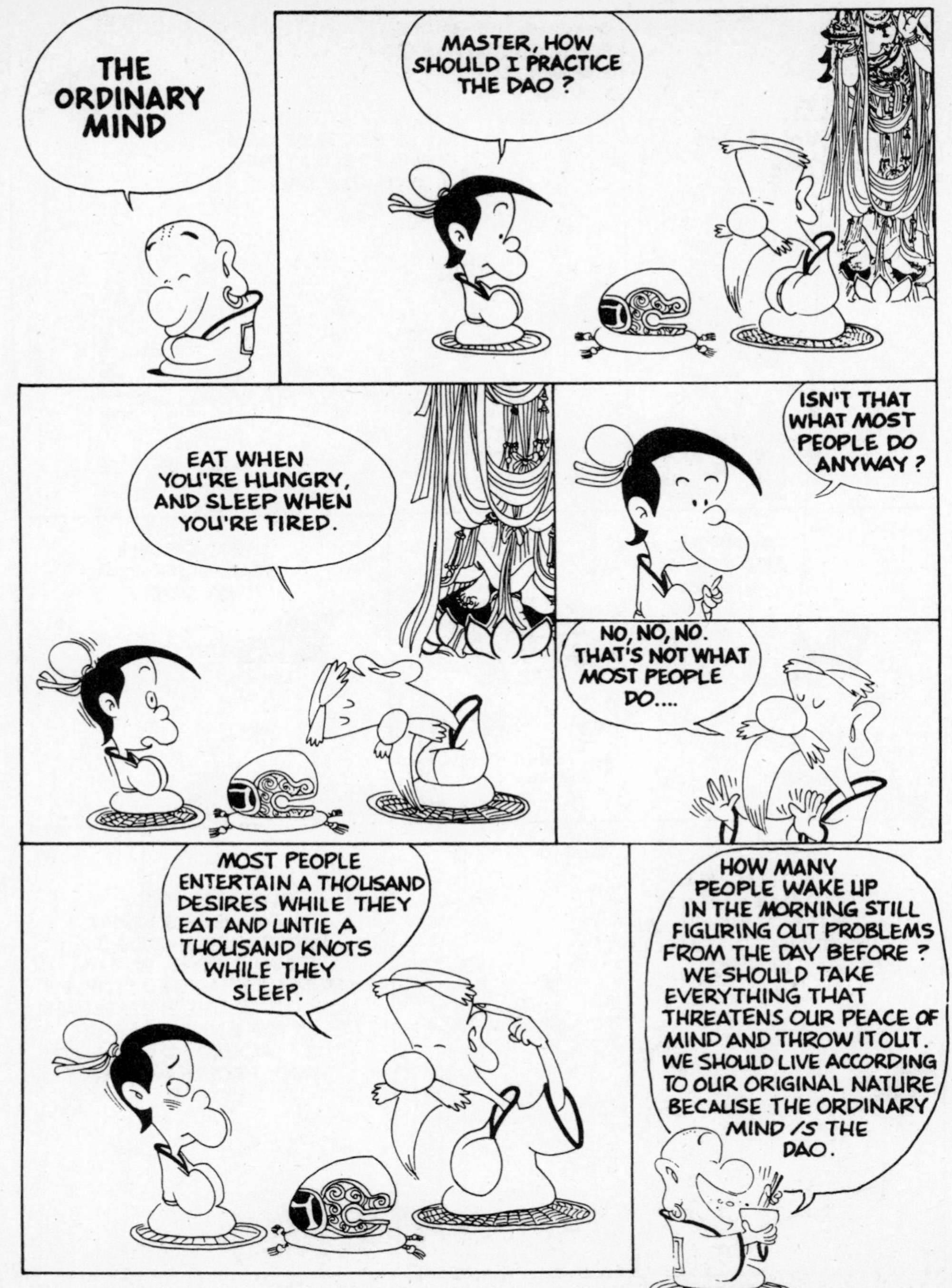

WHAT'S NOT A PRIME CUT ?
ONE DAY WHILE THE MONK PANSHAN WAS WALKING DOWN THE STREET, HE SAW SOME PEOPLE BUYING MEAT OFF A WILD BOAR....
I'D LIKE A POUND OF PRIME MEAT.
ON THIS PORKER, WHAT'S NOT A PRIME CUT ?
!
WHEN PANSHAN HEARD THE BUTCHER'S WORDS, HE FINALLY ATTAINED ENLIGHTENMENT.
ANY TIME AND ANY PLACE ARE ALWAYS THE BEST TIME AND THE BEST PLACE. ALL YOU HAVE TO DO IS EXPERIENCE THINGS WITH AN ATTENTIVE MIND.

幽州盤山寶積禪師，一天路過市場，偶然聽到如下的一段對話而有所悟：
顧客向屠夫説道：「精底割一斤來！」
屠夫放下屠刀叉手道：「老兄，哪個不是精底？」

山谷一日參晦堂和尚，堂云：「公所諳書中，有一兩句，仲尼曰：「二三子以我為隱乎？吾無隱乎爾！」甚與宗門事恰好也，公知之麼？」山谷云：「不知。」後晦堂與山谷山行之次，天香滿山。堂問曰：「公聞木樨花香麼？」云：「聞。」堂曰：「吾無隱乎爾！」山谷釋然有省。經兩月後，參死心禪師，死心一揆云：「長老死，學士死，燒作兩堆灰，恁麼時向什麼處相見？」山擬議，不契。後左官黔南，道力愈勝，於無思念中頓明死心所問，從是得大自在之三昧。

THE SWEET SMELL OF OSMANTHUS
WHAT, AFTER ALL, IS THE PROFOUND MEANING OF ZEN?
CONFUCIUS SAID: "I CONCEAL NOTHING FROM YOU." ZEN DOESN'T HIDE ANYTHING FROM YOU EITHER.
I STILL DON'T GET IT.
COME WITH ME TO THE BACK SIDE OF THIS MOUNTAIN....
CAN YOU SMELL THE SWEET OSMANTHUS?
YES
!
SEE, I'M NOT HIDING ANYTHING FROM YOU EITHER.
SEIZE THE MOMENT: EXPERIENCE THE PRESENT: DON'T LET ANYTHING SLIP BY. EVERY EVENING IS A SPRING EVENING, AND EVERY DAY IS A GOOD DAY.

至江陵白馬寺，堂中遇一老宿，名曰慧勤，師親近詢請。勤曰：「吾久侍丹霞，今既垂老，倦於提誘，汝可往謁翠微，彼即吾同參也。」師禮辭而去，造於翠微之堂。問：「如何是西來的的意？」翠微曰：「待無人即向汝說。」師良久曰：「無人也，請師說。」翠微下禪牀引師入竹園，師又曰：「無人也，請和尚說。」翠微指竹曰：「這竿得恁麼長，那竿得恁麼短。」師雖領其微言，猶未徹其玄旨。

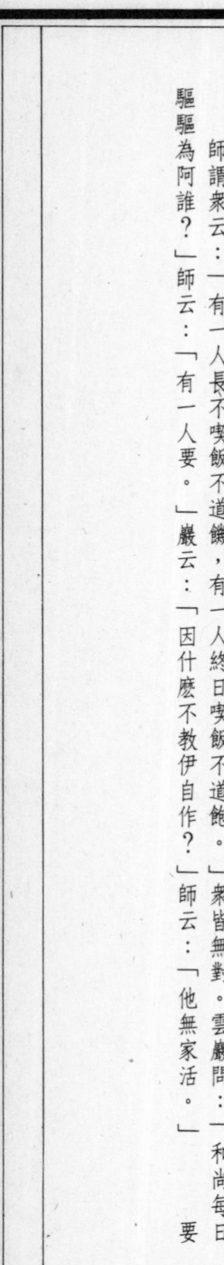
師謂衆云：「有一人長不喫飯不道饑，有一人終日喫飯不道飽。」衆皆無對。雲巖問：「和尚每日驅驅為阿誰？」師云：「有一人要。」巖云：「因什麼不教伊自作？」師云：「他無家活。」

要

NO SELF, NO OTHERS

ONE DAY, YUNYAN WENT TO VISIT AN OLDER MASTER, THE MONK BAIZHANG....

YOU SWEAT AND TOIL LIKE THIS EVERY DAY. WHO ARE YOU DOING IT FOR ?

THERE'S SOMEONE WHO NEEDS IT.

WELL, WHY DON'T YOU TELL THAT PERSON TO DO IT HIMSELF?

HE CAN'T GET ALONG BY HIMSELF.

!

DISTINGUISHING BETWEEN "SELF" AND "OTHER" IS THE SOURCE OF SUFFERING. INSTEAD, WE SHOULD USE THE COMPASSIONATE MIND, WHICH DOES NOT DISTINGUISH BETWEEN SELF AND OTHERS, TO HELP THOSE WHO NEED HELP THE MOST.

師煎茶次，道吾問：「煎與阿誰？」師曰：「有一人要。」曰：「何不教伊自煎？」師曰：「幸有某甲在。」

鏡清問僧：「門外是什麼聲？」僧云：「雨滴聲！」清云：「衆生顛倒，迷己逐物。」僧云：「和尚作麼生？」清云：「泊不迷己。」僧云：「泊不迷己，意旨如何？」清云：「出身猶可易，脱體道應難。」

NOT RECOGNIZING THE TRUE SELF
ONCE AN OFFICIAL NAMED WEI WENT TO SEE THE ZEN MASTER XUANSHA....
PEOPLE SAY THAT WE'RE ALWAYS USING IT, BUT I STILL DON'T KNOW WHAT "IT" IS.
HERE, FIRST HAVE SOME MELON SEEDS.
THANK YOU!
CRACK!
UH, MASTER? YOU STILL HAVEN'T TOLD ME WHAT "IT" IS.
IT'S THIS! YOU HAVE IT EVERY DAY, AND YET YOU DON'T KNOW WHAT "IT" IS!
"ARRIVING AT THE DAO IS NOT DIFFICULT. WHAT'S LEFT IS CHOOSING IT." ASKING WHERE THE ROAD LIES IS A GREAT MISTAKE BECAUSE THERE IS NO ROAD. WE HAVE BEEN ON THE WAY (THE DAO) ALL ALONG.

師與韋監軍喫果子，韋問：「如何是日用而不知」?師（玄沙）拈起果子曰：「喫」。韋喫果子了，再問之，師曰：「只者是日用而不知」。

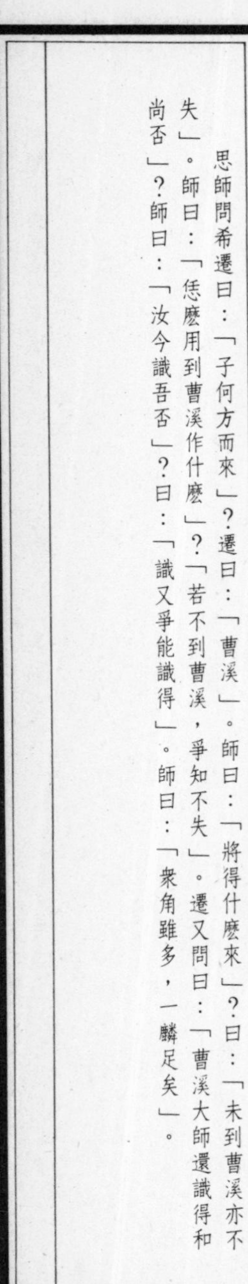

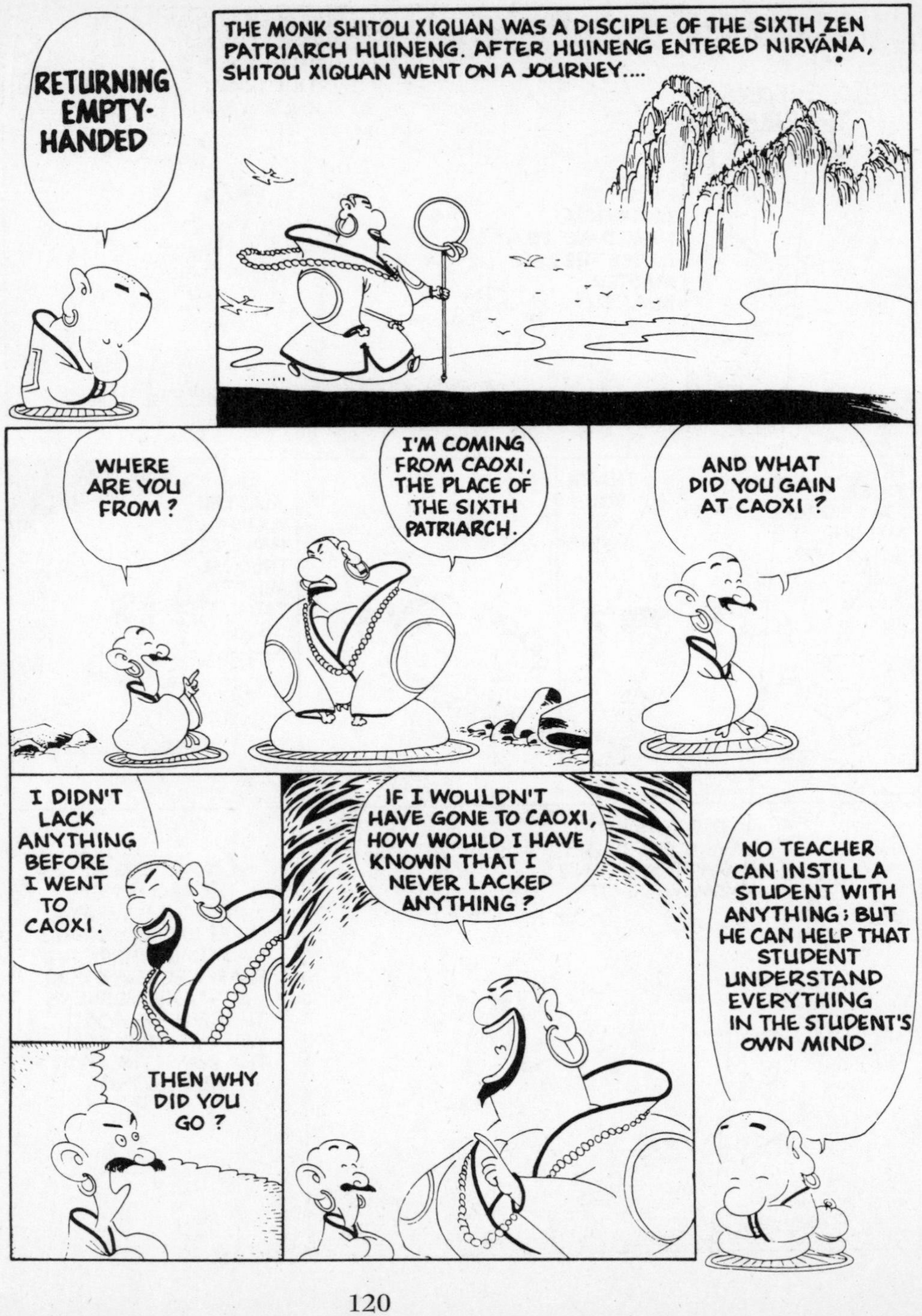

思師問希遷曰：「子何方而來」？遷曰：「曹溪」。師曰：「將得什麼來」？曰：「未到曹溪亦不失」。師曰：「恁麼用到曹溪作什麼」？「若不到曹溪，爭知不失」。遷又問曰：「曹溪大師還識得和尚否」？師曰：「汝今識吾否」？曰：「識又爭能識得」。師曰：「衆角雖多，一麟足矣」。

RETURNING EMPTY-HANDED

THE MONK SHITOU XIQUAN WAS A DISCIPLE OF THE SIXTH ZEN PATRIARCH HUINENG. AFTER HUINENG ENTERED NIRVĀṆA, SHITOU XIQUAN WENT ON A JOURNEY....

WHERE ARE YOU FROM?

I'M COMING FROM CAOXI, THE PLACE OF THE SIXTH PATRIARCH.

AND WHAT DID YOU GAIN AT CAOXI?

I DIDN'T LACK ANYTHING BEFORE I WENT TO CAOXI.

THEN WHY DID YOU GO?

IF I WOULDN'T HAVE GONE TO CAOXI, HOW WOULD I HAVE KNOWN THAT I NEVER LACKED ANYTHING?

NO TEACHER CAN INSTILL A STUDENT WITH ANYTHING; BUT HE CAN HELP THAT STUDENT UNDERSTAND EVERYTHING IN THE STUDENT'S OWN MIND.

禪的源底，究非語言可得表現；禪的真實相，不容有閒言語、閒妄想的餘地。除「教外別傳，不立文字，直指人心，見性成佛」之外，別無可求之道。不立，即是直示着不容語言文字，原來怎樣就是怎樣地直接啓示着真理。

師住西堂後，有一俗士問：「有天堂地獄否？」師曰：「有。」曰：「有佛法僧寶否？」師曰：「有。」更有多問，盡答言有曰：「和尚恁麼道莫錯否？」師曰：「汝曾見曾宿來耶？」曰：「某甲曾參徑山和尚來。」師曰：「徑山向汝作麼生道？」曰：「他道一切總無。」師曰：「汝有妻否？」曰：「有。」師曰：「徑山和尚有妻否？」曰：「無。」師曰：「徑山和尚道無即得。」俗士禮謝而去。

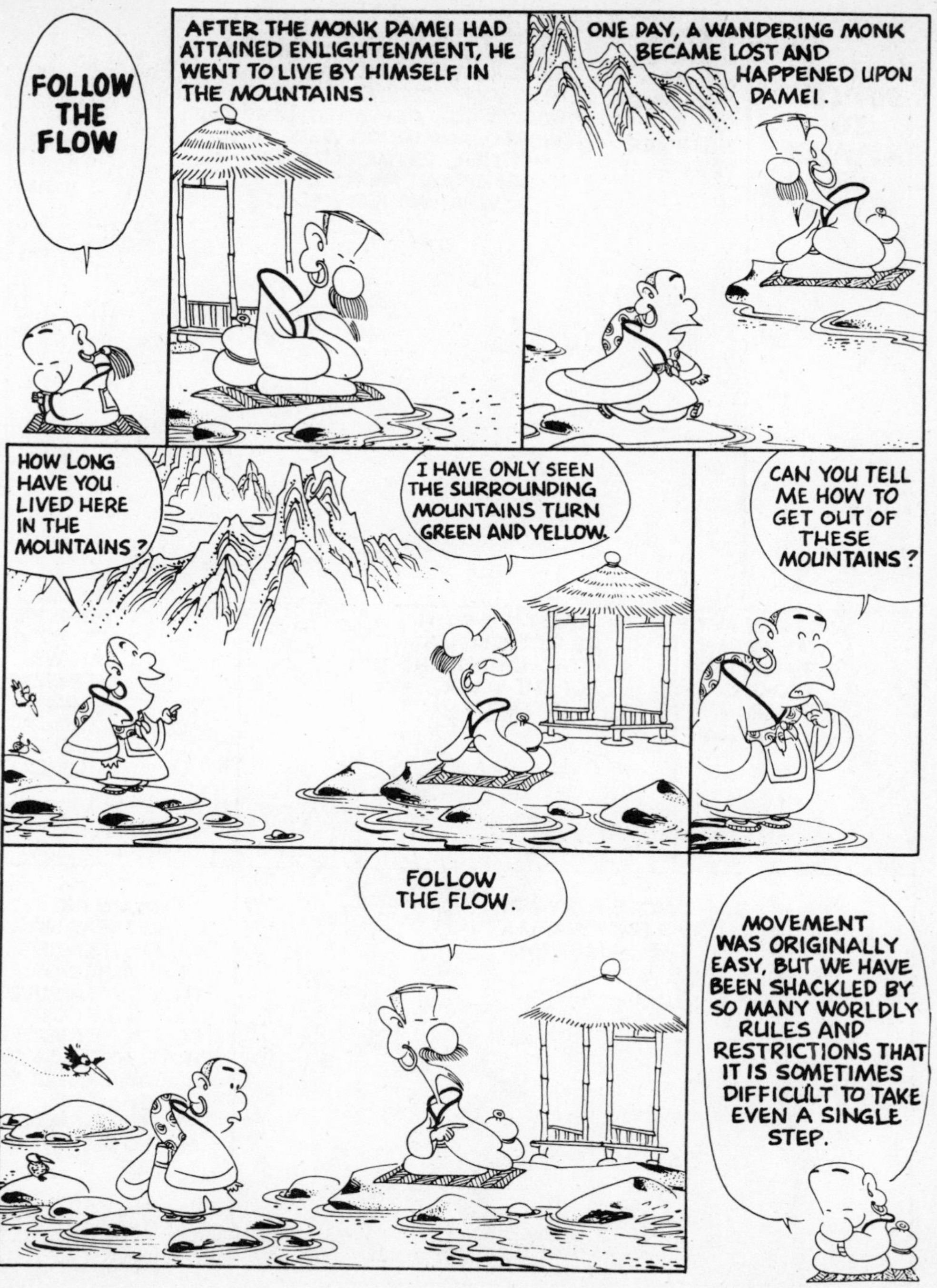

FOLLOW THE FLOW
AFTER THE MONK DAMEI HAD ATTAINED ENLIGHTENMENT, HE WENT TO LIVE BY HIMSELF IN THE MOUNTAINS.
ONE DAY, A WANDERING MONK BECAME LOST AND HAPPENED UPON DAMEI.
HOW LONG HAVE YOU LIVED HERE IN THE MOUNTAINS?
I HAVE ONLY SEEN THE SURROUNDING MOUNTAINS TURN GREEN AND YELLOW.
CAN YOU TELL ME HOW TO GET OUT OF THESE MOUNTAINS?
FOLLOW THE FLOW.
MOVEMENT WAS ORIGINALLY EASY, BUT WE HAVE BEEN SHACKLED BY SO MANY WORLDLY RULES AND RESTRICTIONS THAT IT IS SOMETIMES DIFFICULT TO TAKE EVEN A SINGLE STEP.

師即大悟。唐貞元中，居於大梅山鄞縣南七十里梅子真舊隱，時鹽官會下一僧入山採柱杖，迷路至庵所問曰：「和尚在此山來多少時也？」師曰：「只見四山青又黃。」又問：「出山路向什麼處去？」師曰：「隨流去。」

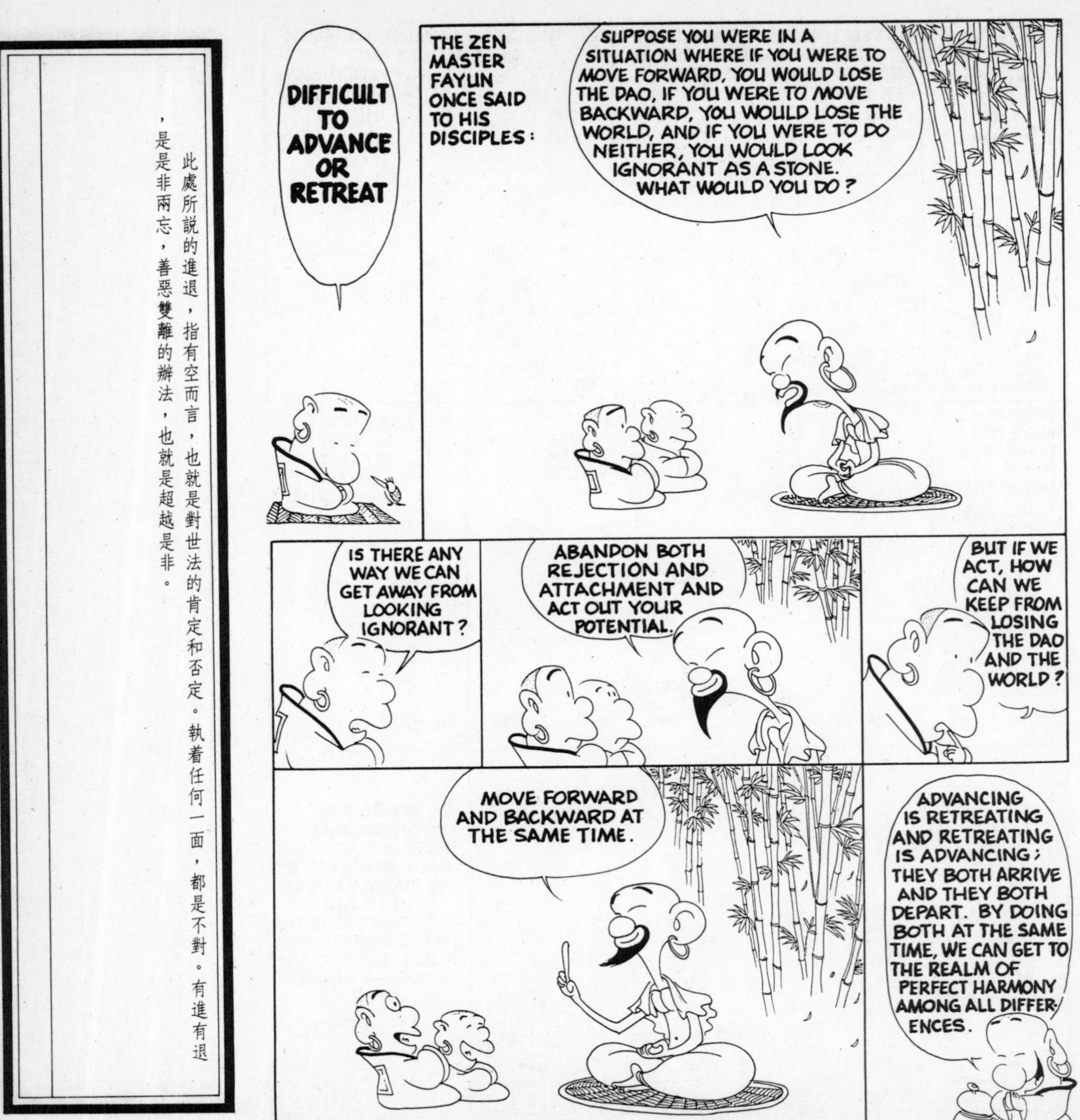
此處所說的進退，指有空而言，也就是對世法的肯定和否定。執着任何一面，都是不對。有進有退，是是非兩忘，善惡雙離的辦法，也就是超越是非。
DIFFICULT TO ADVANCE OR RETREAT
THE ZEN MASTER FAYUN ONCE SAID TO HIS DISCIPLES:
SUPPOSE YOU WERE IN A SITUATION WHERE IF YOU WERE TO MOVE FORWARD, YOU WOULD LOSE THE DAO, IF YOU WERE TO MOVE BACKWARD, YOU WOULD LOSE THE WORLD, AND IF YOU WERE TO DO NEITHER, YOU WOULD LOOK IGNORANT AS A STONE. WHAT WOULD YOU DO?
IS THERE ANY WAY WE CAN GET AWAY FROM LOOKING IGNORANT?
ABANDON BOTH REJECTION AND ATTACHMENT AND ACT OUT YOUR POTENTIAL.
BUT IF WE ACT, HOW CAN WE KEEP FROM LOSING THE DAO AND THE WORLD?
MOVE FORWARD AND BACKWARD AT THE SAME TIME.
ADVANCING IS RETREATING AND RETREATING IS ADVANCING; THEY BOTH ARRIVE AND THEY BOTH DEPART. BY DOING BOTH AT THE SAME TIME, WE CAN GET TO THE REALM OF PERFECT HARMONY AMONG ALL DIFFERENCES.

NO BETTER THAN A CLOWN
THE MONK SHOUDUAN OF BAIYUN WAS VERY INDUSTRIOUS BUT LACKED A SENSE OF HUMOR.
HIS TEACHER YANGQI ONCE ASKED HIM:
WHO WAS YOUR PREVIOUS TEACHER?
THE MONK CHALING YU.
I HEARD THAT MONK YU WAS ENLIGHTENED WHEN HE SLIPPED ON A BRIDGE AND FELL INTO THE WATER. HE EVEN WROTE A POEM ABOUT IT.
YES, HE DID, AND I STILL REMEMBER IT.
I HAVE A PEARL BRIGHT AND SHINY,
LONG OBSCURED BY DUST AND FILTH;
NOW THE DUST IS GONE AND BRIGHTNESS BORN,
ILLUMINATING THE RIVERS AND HILLS.
HA-HA HA-HA!
? ?

守端有一次對楊岐口述郁和尚的悟道偈：「我有明珠一顆，久被塵勞關鎖。今朝塵盡光生，照破河山萬朵」。楊岐聽了笑着走了。守端整夜失眠。次日問楊岐為何大笑？楊答：「你不如小丑，小丑喜歡人笑，你却怕人笑」。守端因而大悟。小丑能使人笑，是小丑演技的成功。至於楊岐的笑。有兩種看法：一種是因守端轉述他人的知見，等於數他家珍寶，與己何益。故此發笑。一種是守端既是欣賞這個偈子，是已理悟心即是佛的道理。所以楊岐笑着走了，好讓守端懷疑，繼續參究。果然守端苦參一夜以後

，靈機活躍；再經楊岐一言，便開悟了。楊岐之言，也暗含着只要自己有了真功夫，笑罵由人，與我何損。正老子所謂：「不笑不足為道」。一切但求之在我而已。所謂「自得之則資之深，資之深則取諸左右逢其源」。又何必捨己求人。（引自周中一「禪話」）

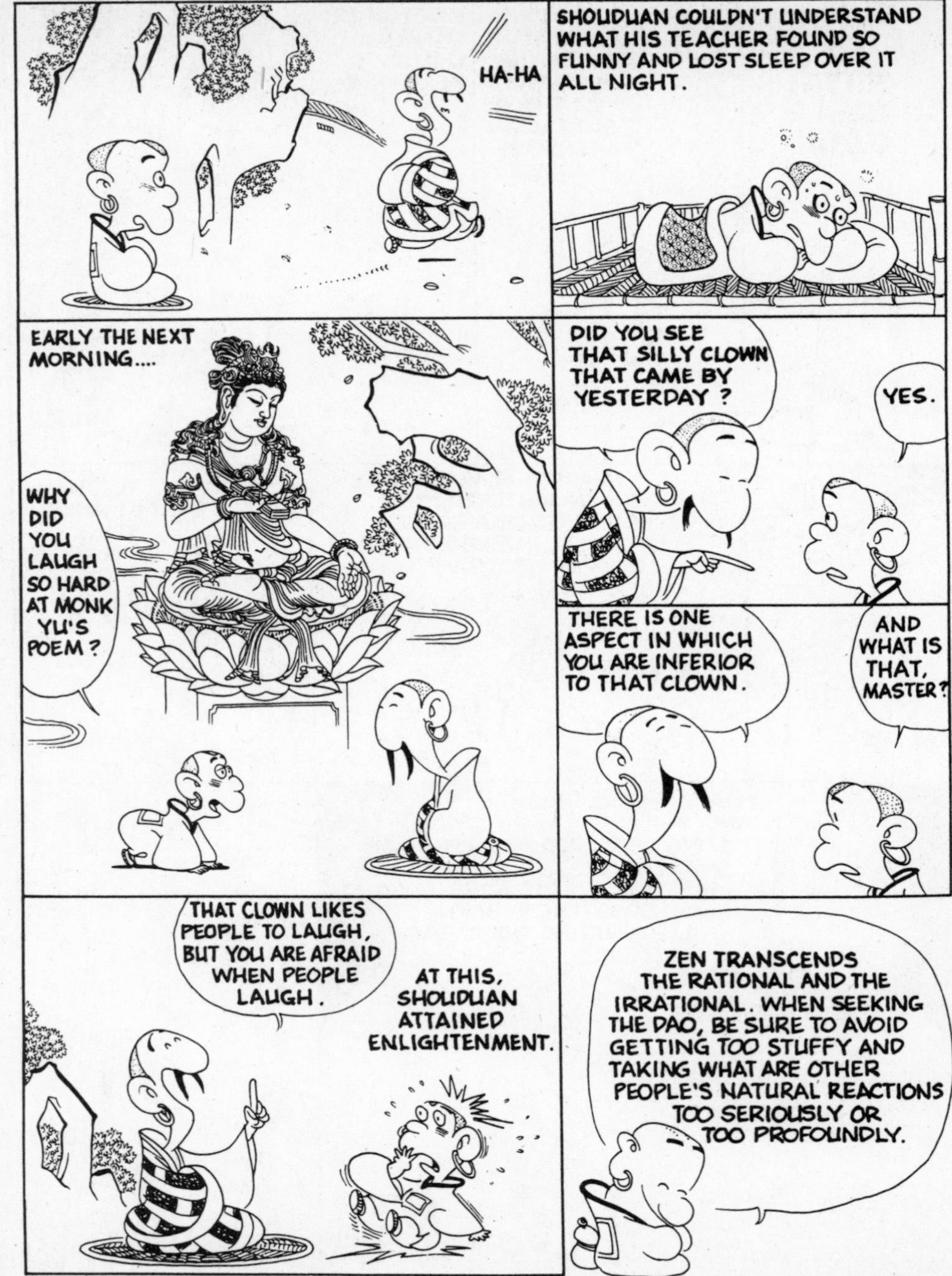

DANXIA BURNS THE BUDDHA
ONCE WHILE THE ZEN MASTER DANXIA WAS STUDYING AT THE HUILIN TEMPLE, THE WEATHER WAS BITTER COLD, SO TO KEEP WARM, HE BURNED A STATUE OF THE BUDDHA....
YOU CRETIN! HOW COULD YOU BURN A STATUE OF THE BUDDHA?!
I WANTED TO SEE IF ANY ŚARĪRA * WOULD COME OUT....
WHY WOULD THERE BE ŚARĪRA IN A WOODEN STATUE?
HUH?...
WELL, IF THERE AREN'T ANY ŚARĪRA, BRING THEM ALL DOWN HERE TO BURN!
A MAN OF THE DAO IS OF NO-MIND; HOW CAN HE DO WRONG? BY NOT GETTING MIRED IN APPEARANCES AND BY FOLLOWING OUR ORIGINAL NATURE, WE CAN DO NO WRONG.

唐元和中，（丹霞）至洛京龍門、香山，與伏牛（自在）和尚為莫逆之友。後於慧林寺，遇天大寒，，師取木佛焚之，人或譏之。師曰：「吾燒取舍利」。人曰：「木頭何有」？師曰：「若爾者，何責我乎」？

* ŚARĪRA: A SMALL, IMMUTABLE RELIC SAID TO BE LEFT OVER AFTER THE CREMATION OF THE BODY OF A BUDDHA

◉吴怡先生認為：在這則公案裏，丹霞以一位禪師的身份，居然親自燒木佛以取暖，這在一般宗教的眼中，無異是叛教的行為，可是在禪宗的文獻裏却大書特書，變成了一則著名的公案。究竟是何原因？如果我們依照這則公案的對話來看，問題似乎很簡單，因為木佛沒有舍利、所以可焚；也就是說木佛只是偶像，沒有佛性，所以能燒。這種行為在禪宗的文獻裏，並不希奇，像呵佛罵祖之事，經常出現。其目的都是要我們打破心中的執着……，這種焚木佛的境界固然很高，但其行為却只許丹霞有一次；丹霞自己用多了，或後人盲目的模倣，都將變為狂禪。

HOW CAN I GET THE MOUNTAINS, THE RIVERS, AND THE GREAT EARTH TO RETURN TO ME ?

YOU SHOULD RETURN YOURSELF TO THE MOUNTAINS, THE RIVERS, AND THE GREAT EARTH !

IF YOU TRY TO ATTRACT THE TRUTH THROUGH THE SELF, THEN YOU'VE YET TO COMPLETELY ABANDON THE SELF, AND YOU'LL NEVER GET TO THE COMPLETE TRUTH. ONLY BY ASSIMILATING YOURSELF WITH NATURE AND SINCERELY FORGETTING THE SELF CAN YOU BE ONE WITH THE TRUTH.

僧問揚州石塔宣秘禮禪師：「山河大地，與己是同是別」？師曰「長亭涼夜月，多為客鋪舒」。一切自然環境，與衆生皆有深切的關係。皆能影響衆生的生活。故天地並生，萬物為一體。

僧問大龍：「色身敗壞，如何是堅固法身？」龍云：「山花開似錦，澗水湛如藍。」
MOUNTAIN FLOWERS BLOSSOM LIKE BROCADE
MASTER, ALL TANGIBLE THINGS WILL PASS AWAY, BUT IS THERE AN ETERNAL TRUTH ?
YES, THERE IS.
LIKE WILDFLOWERS THAT BLOOM SO BEAUTIFULLY, RESEMBLING A SILK BROCADE.
LIKE A SEEMINGLY STILL STREAM THAT IS ACTUALLY FLOWING.
FLOWERS ARE QUICK TO WITHER, YET THE CYCLE WILL ALWAYS REMAIN; WATER MAY MOVE, BUT THE SURFACE OF THE STREAM WILL NEVER CHANGE. THE MEANING OF LIFE LIES IN THE PROCESS OF LIVING--CHANGE IS THE ONLY THING THAT NEVER CHANGES.

WHAT ISN'T THE BUDDHA-DHARMA
AS A DISCIPLE WAS TAKING LEAVE OF THE MONK NIAOWO....
THANK YOU VERY MUCH FOR EVERYTHING. I'LL BE GOING NOW.
WHERE ARE YOU OFF TO?
I'M GOING TO TRAVEL THE LAND STUDYING THE BUDDHA-DHARMA.
SPEAKING OF THE BUDDHA-DHARMA, I HAVE A BIT OF IT RIGHT HERE....
WHERE?
AT THIS, NIAOWO PULLED A THREAD FROM HIS SLEEVE....
!
IS THIS NOT THE BUDDHA-DHARMA AS WELL?
THE TRUTH OF THINGS DOES NOT RESIDE IN SOME UNREACHABLE, DISTANT PLACE; IT IS IN OUR MINDS. EVERYTHING POSSESSES THE BUDDHA-NATURE, SO WHAT IS THERE THAT ISN'T THE BUDDHA-DHARMA?

有侍者會通，唐德宗時為六宮使，王族咸美之。七歲蔬食，十一受五戒，二十有二為出家故休官，鳥窠即與披剃，其常卯齋，晝夜精進，誦大乘經而習安般三昧。忽一日，欲辭去，師問曰：「汝今何往」？對曰：「會通為法出家，以和尚不垂慈誨，今往諸方學佛法去」。師曰：「若是佛法，吾此間亦有少許」。曰：「如何是和尚佛法」？師於身上拈起布毛吹之，會通遂領悟玄旨。時謂布毛侍者。

師問西堂：「汝還解捉得虛空麼？」西堂云：「捉得！」師云：「作麼生捉？」堂以手撮虛空師云
：「作麼生恁麼捉虛空？」堂却問：「師兄作麼生捉？」師把西堂鼻孔拽西堂作忍痛聲云：「大殺拽人
鼻孔。」直得脱去師云：「直須恁麼捉虛空始得。」
GRASPING EMPTINESS
SHIGONG ASKED A YOUNGER MASTER, XITANG ZHICANG:
CAN YOU GRAB AHOLD OF EMPTINESS?
SURE.
WELL, LET'S SEE YOU DO IT.
OKAY.
IS THAT IT? YOU DIDN'T GET ANYTHING!
THEN HOW WOULD YOU DO IT?
LIKE THIS!
OW! THAT HURTS! THAT HURTS!
SINCE MATTER IS EMPTY, AND EMPTINESS IS MATTER, GRABBING A PIECE OF EMPTINESS ISN'T AS CLOSE TO REALITY AS JUST REACHING OUT AND GRABBING THE OTHER PERSON'S NOSE IS.

THE FIRE GOD SEEKING FIRE
XUANZE ASKED THE MONK QINGFENG:
WHAT IS THE BUDDHA?
THE FIRE GOD COMES SEEKING FIRE.
!
HA-HA! I GET IT! I GET IT!
I FINALLY UNDERSTAND!
WHAT DID YOU LEARN FROM QINGFENG?
THE FIRE GOD IS FIRE, YET HE SEEKS FIRE FROM SOMEONE ELSE. JUST LIKE I'M THE BUDDHA, AND YET I WENT TO SOMEBODY ELSE TO ASK ABOUT THE BUDDHA.

在外道問佛的公案（第六十五）中：

『外道問佛：「不問有言，不問無言。」世尊良久。外道讚嘆云：「大慈大悲，開我迷雲，令我得入！」外道去後，阿難問佛：「外道有何所證，而言『得入』？」佛言：「如世良馬，見鞭影而行。」』

這個公案外道的問，據語錄原文：「外道問佛：如何是佛？但不問有言，不問無言」的節記。這個質問，就是說：所謂佛，是什麼呢？換句話說：釋尊大悟的內容，是什麼東西呢？意即：不是問超越的

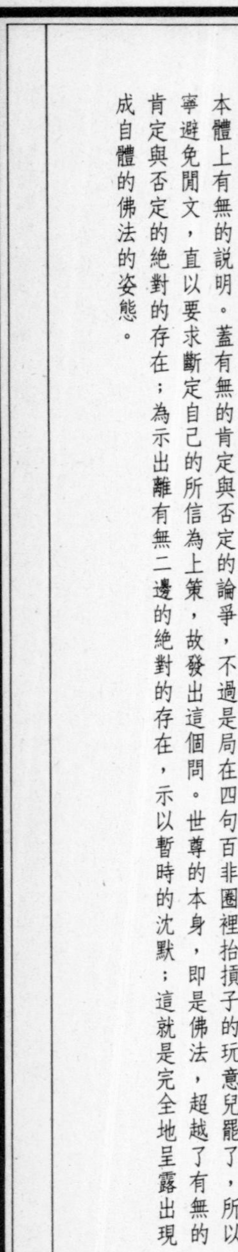

本體上有無的説明。蓋有無的肯定與否定的論爭，不過是局在四句百非圈裡抬摃子的玩意兒罷了，所以寧避免聞文，直以要求斷定自己的所信為上策，故發出這個問。世尊的本身，即是佛法，超越了有無的肯定與否定的絶對的存在；為示出離有無二邊的絶對的存在，示以暫時的沈默；這就是完全地呈露出現成自體的佛法的姿態。

乾峰和尚因僧問：「十方薄伽梵，一路涅槃門。未審路頭在甚麼處？」峰拈起拄杖劃一劃云：「在者裏！」後僧請益雲門，門拈起扇子云：「扇子踍跳上三十三天，築着帝釋鼻孔，東海鯉魚打一棒，雨似盆傾！」

無門曰：一人向深深海底行，簸土揚塵；一人於高高山頂立，白浪滔天。把定放行，各出一隻手扶豎宗乘，大似兩個駝子相撞着，世上應無直底人。正眼觀來，二大老總未識路頭在。

僧問：「寒暑到來，如何回避？」師云：「何不向無寒暑處去？」云：「如何是無寒暑處？」師云
：「寒時寒殺闍黎，熱時熱殺闍黎。」
投子同云：「幾乎與麼去。」
COLD WHEN COLD, HOT WHEN HOT
A STUDENT ASKED LIANGJIE (LIANG-CHIEH) OF DONGSHAN (TUNG-SHAN):
WHERE SHOULD WE GO FOR SHELTER DURING SUMMER AND WINTER?
WHY DON'T YOU GO SOMEPLACE WHERE THERE IS NO SUMMER AND WINTER?
WHERE IS THERE A PLACE THAT IS NEITHER HOT NOR COLD?
WHEN IT'S COLD OUT, TURN YOURSELF COLD.
WHEN IT'S HOT OUT, TURN YOURSELF HOT.
IF WE ARE COMFORTABLE IN ZEN, HEAT AND COLD WON'T BOTHER US. WINTER AND SUMMER ARE NATURAL OCCURRENCES, SO WE SHOULD BECOME ONE WITH THEM RATHER THAN FIGHT THEM; THEN THEY WILL SUDDENLY DISAPPEAR.

尼衆問：「如何得為僧去」？師曰：「作尼來多少時也」？尼曰：「還有為僧時也無」？師曰：「汝即今是什麼」？尼曰：「現是尼身，何得不識」？師曰：「誰識汝」？

洞山和尚因僧問：「如何是佛？」山云：「麻三斤！」

無門曰：洞山老人參得些蚌蛤禪，纔開兩片，露出肝腸。然雖如是，且道：向什麼處見洞山？頌曰：突出麻三斤，言親意更親。來說是非者，便是是非人！

◉蚌蛤禪：言其禪直接明白，如蚌蛤一般，纔一開口，便表露無遺也。

◉突然提出「麻三斤」來答「如何是佛」的問話，此答不但言語親切，而且意思亦更加的親切，毫無隔閡。此事沒有是非可說，來說是非的人，便是生是惹非的人了。

宇宙萬有，是無常的，也是無始無終的存在着。現象即實在，眼見耳聞都是佛。僧問「如何是佛」？答之以「麻三斤」，也是舉其一例罷了。這個公案語，不是這樣就完結。僧於洞山之答不能理解，再舉以問智門。智門答以「花簇簇，錦簇簇」，轉問僧曰：「會不會」？僧說：「不會」。因之更說云：「南地竹兮北地木」。這是說：黃花、紅葉、竹、木、無不是佛。由此類推三斤麻，亦自然是佛了。（引自芝峯法師譯「禪學講話」）

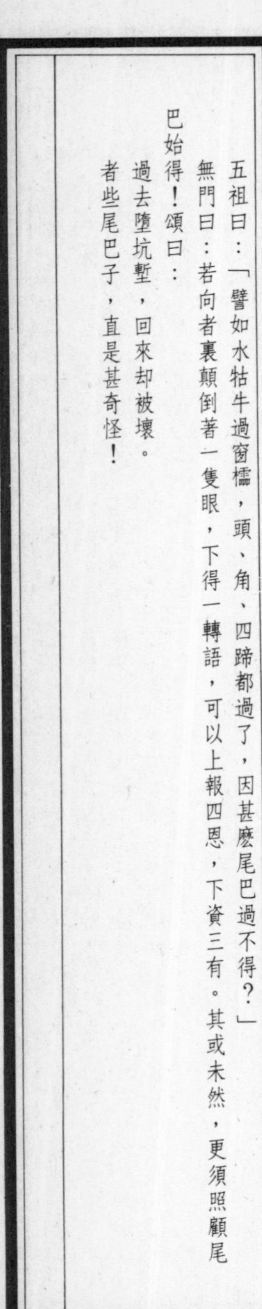
五祖曰：「譬如水牯牛過窗櫺，頭、角、四蹄都過了，因甚麼尾巴過不得？」

無門曰：若向者裏顛倒著一隻眼，下得一轉語，可以上報四恩，下資三有。其或未然，更須照顧尾巴始得！頌曰：

過去墮坑塹，回來却被壞。

者些尾巴子，直是甚奇怪！

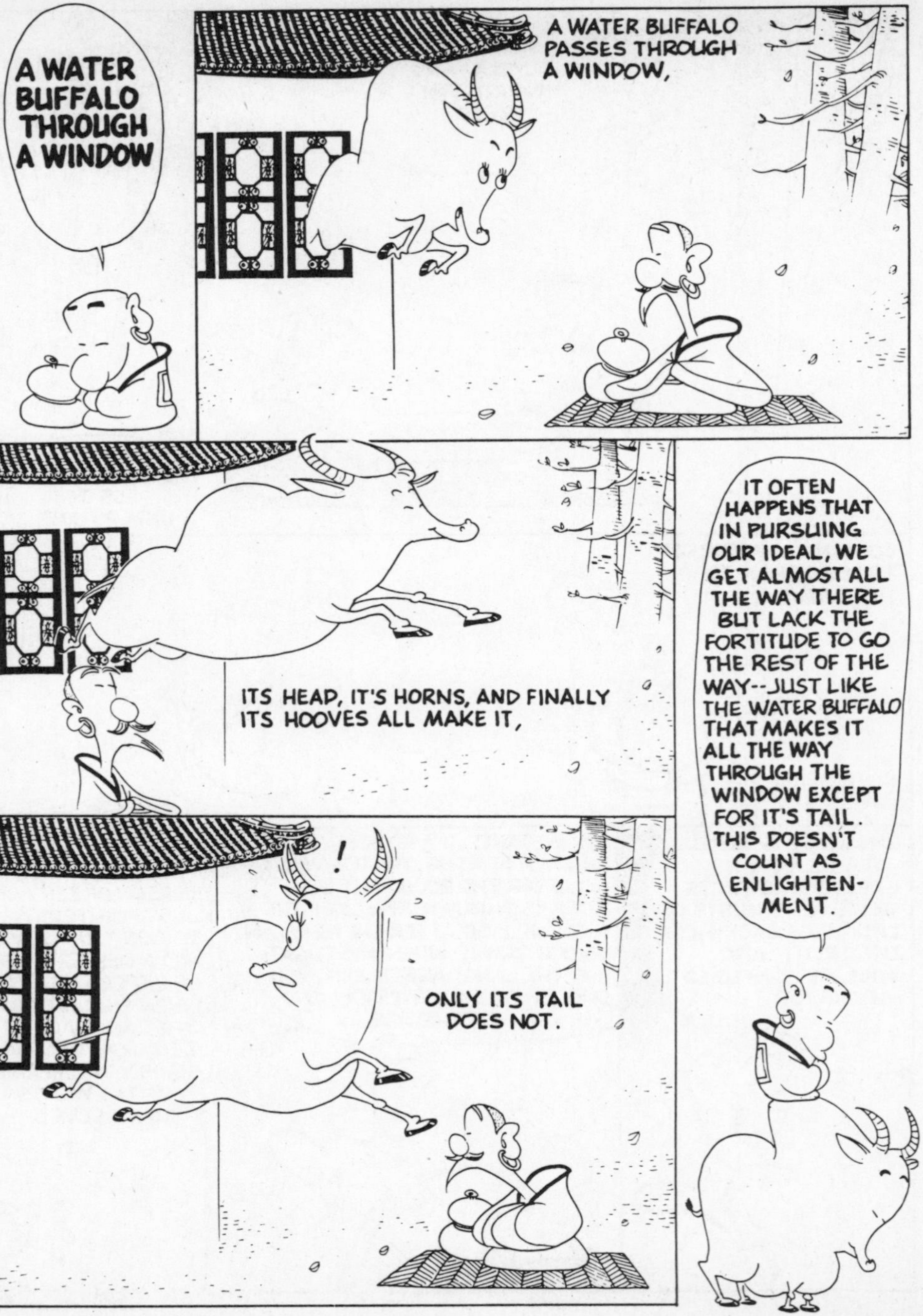

A WATER BUFFALO THROUGH A WINDOW

A WATER BUFFALO PASSES THROUGH A WINDOW,

ITS HEAD, IT'S HORNS, AND FINALLY ITS HOOVES ALL MAKE IT,

ONLY ITS TAIL DOES NOT.

IT OFTEN HAPPENS THAT IN PURSUING OUR IDEAL, WE GET ALMOST ALL THE WAY THERE BUT LACK THE FORTITUDE TO GO THE REST OF THE WAY--JUST LIKE THE WATER BUFFALO THAT MAKES IT ALL THE WAY THROUGH THE WINDOW EXCEPT FOR IT'S TAIL. THIS DOESN'T COUNT AS ENLIGHTEN-MENT.

瑯琊覺和尚語錄：「先聖道：『有物先天地，無形本寂寥，能為萬物主，不逐四時彫』。好個頌，却成兩槪。若有人檢點得出，許你具一隻眼」。前兩句說的是體，第三句說的是用。體用分離，所以說是成了兩槪。體用本是不可分的。分成兩槪，則非自性；只是識心中有對待的事物。覺師教人檢點的，當是最後一句。「四時彫」三字是指用而言。上面用「不逐」二字予以否定，是就體而言。一句中有動有靜，體用兼攝，而又相即相離，真是活潑潑的自性，只此五字，說明了體用的超越性。（引自周中一「禪話」）

「景德傳燈錄」另有一則「萬古長空，一朝風月」的對話：

問：「達摩未來此土時，還有佛法也無」。師（天柱崇慧）曰：「未來時且置，即今事作麼生」？曰：「某甲不會，乞師指示」？師曰：「萬古長空，一朝風月」。良久又曰：「闍黎會麼？自己分上作麼生，干他達摩與未來作麼」？

吳怡先生對此則公案有如下的說法：所謂萬古長空，就是指的佛法無邊，無過去、現在、未來，這是真空。所謂一朝風月乃指天地間任何事物，都有其當體的存在，這是妙有。但真空即妙有，妙有即真

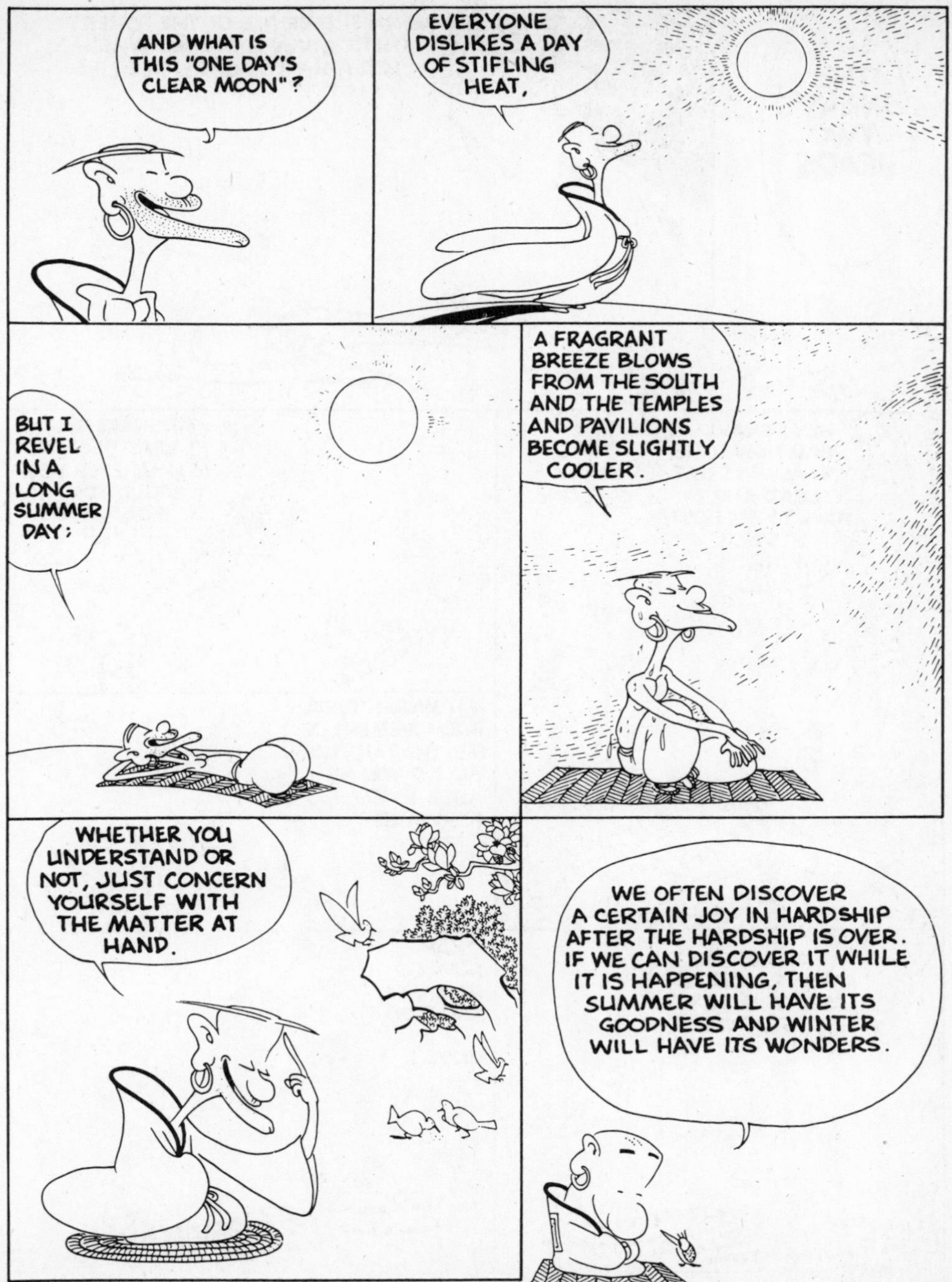

空，萬古是一朝，一朝也是萬古，所以天柱不談「未來」，而只問「今事」，因為「今事」能明，即通

吳怡先生對此則公案有如下的說法：所謂萬古長空，就是指的佛法無邊，無過去、現在、未來，這是真空。所謂一朝風月乃是指天地間任何事物，都有其當體的存在，這是妙有。但真空即妙有，妙有即真空，萬古是一朝，一朝也是萬古，所以天柱不談「未來」，而只問「今事」，因為「今事」能明，即通未來。而當下能悟，即是佛性，還管他達摩的來與未來。

溈山靈佑將入滅時語衆云：「老僧百年後向山下作一頭水牯牛，左脅書五字云：「溈山僧某甲。此時喚作溈山僧，又是水牯牛，喚作水牯牛，又是溈山僧。到底喚作什麼即得」？一個人在將死之時，生理上的痛苦，心理上的悲哀，都是免不了的。在此千鈞一髮之際的生死關頭，居然能夠談笑自若。此種超越生死的達觀態度，實足令人驚奇。但令人驚奇的還不在此。尤其是他把自己和水牯牛搭在一起。乍然一聽他的怪論，會使你啼笑皆非。我們再仔細地一推敲，也就覺得平淡無奇。因溈山僧與水牯牛本為

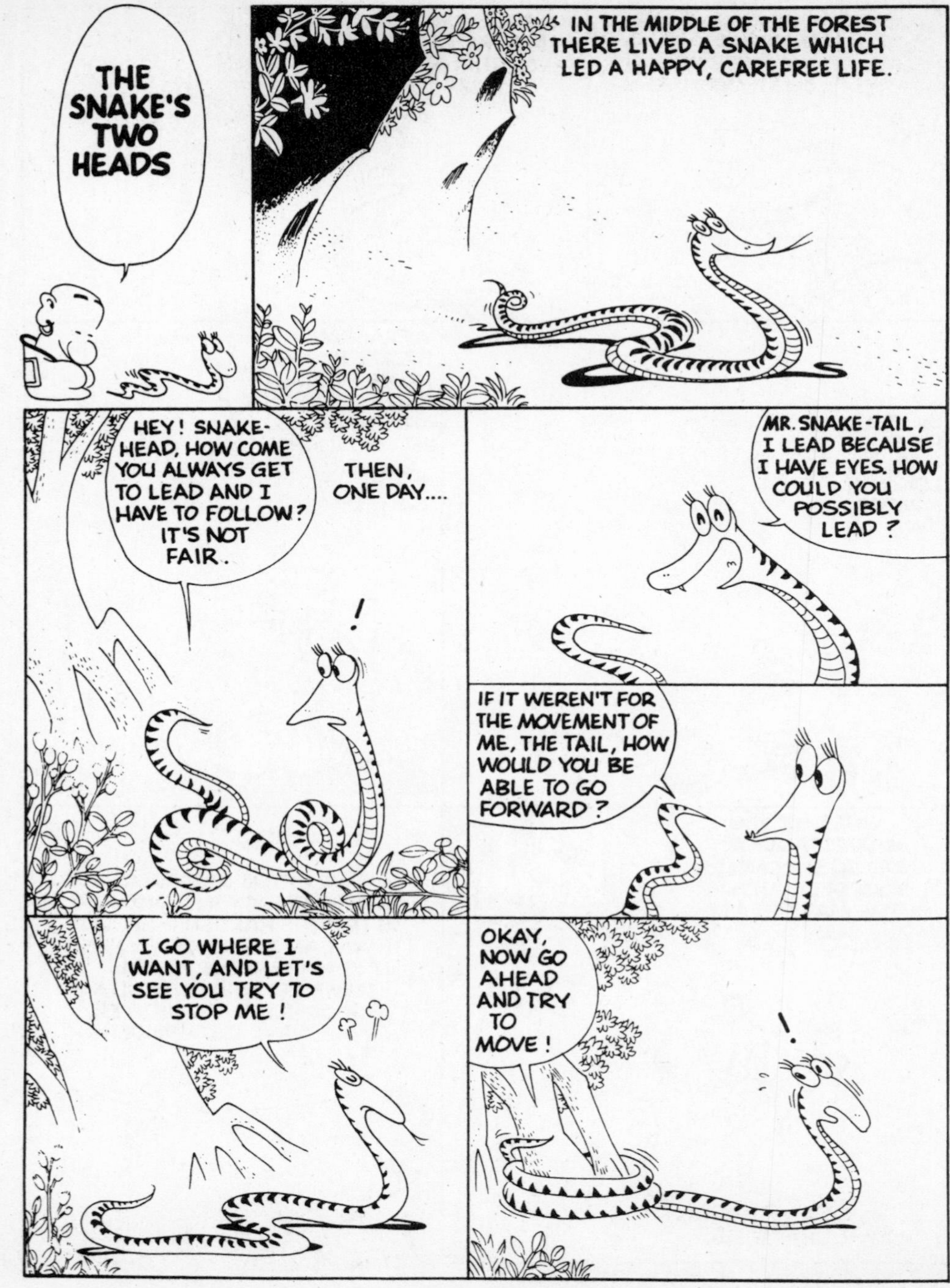

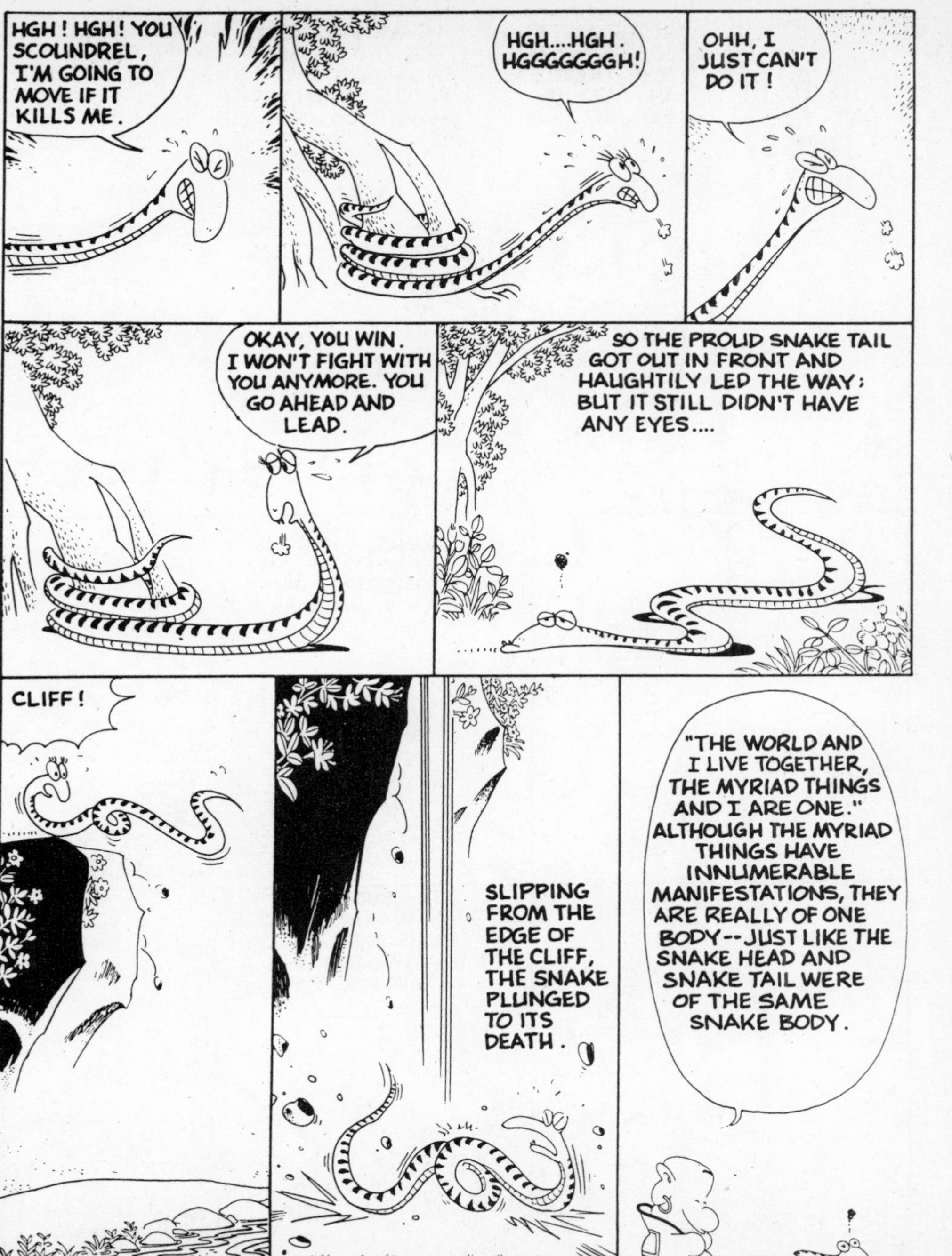

大自然不可分的一體。一個人只要沒有能所的分別心，便能超越自他，超越物我。不僅人與人間，無自他之分，乃至人與畜間，亦無自他之分。一個禪人到此境地，已是外形骸，一生死，所以能夠從容坐化。（引自周中一「禪話」）

SOLILOQUY OF THE FROGS
IN THE LUSH BUSHES BESIDE A SMALL POND THERE LIVED A FAMILY OF FROGS....
HEAVEN IS THERE FOR FROGS, AND EARTH IS THERE FOR FROGS – SO THAT WE HAVE ROOM IN WHICH TO LIVE.
YIPPIE!
YIPPIE! YIPPIE! YIPPIE!
WATER IS THERE FOR FROGS, AND THE AIR IS THERE FOR FROGS.
YIPPIE!
YIPPIE! YIPPIE! YIPPIE!
THE BUGS IN THE AIR ARE THERE FOR FROGS, AND THE FRUIT ON THE GROUND IS THERE FOR FROGS.

大梅問馬祖云：「什麼是佛」？馬祖答：「即心即佛」。大梅言下便悟。後來馬祖派一個僧人去考驗大梅。僧問大梅云：「你在馬祖門下學到些什麼」？大梅回答：「馬祖教我即心即佛」。僧云：「現在馬祖已改變了，說非心非佛」。大梅云：「這個老和尚作弄人沒有了期。管他什麼非心非佛，我只管即心即佛」。僧人歸語馬祖。馬祖便說：「梅子熟了」。這是指大梅已澈悟而言。這段公案說明學人不能執着肯定或否定的一面，要有一種超越是非的精神，才是澈悟。宗寶云：「即心即佛，表語也；非心

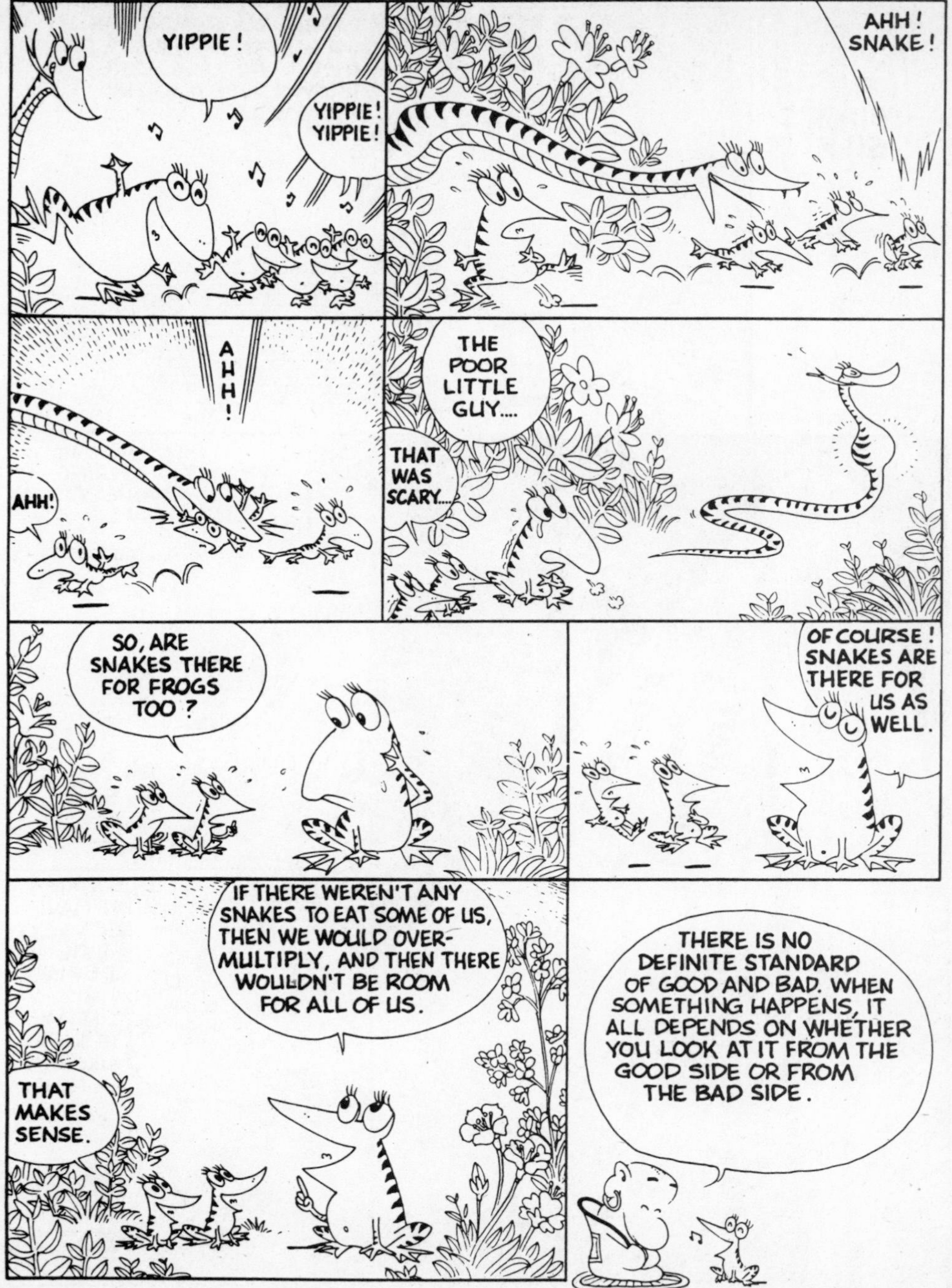

非佛，遮語也。今人多重遮語，謂無痕跡，而忽表語。不知即心即佛，惟過量大人，方能擔荷」。又云：「二祖覓心不可得，達摩云：『與汝安心竟』。與此同一鼻孔」。宗寶所說的表語，即指肯定而言；遮語指否定而言。大梅的表語，正表示能夠擔荷的過量大人。所以馬祖說他成熟了。

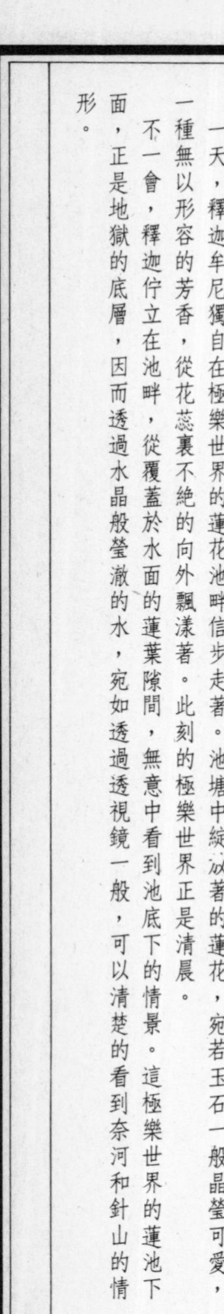

一天，釋迦牟尼獨自在極樂世界的蓮花池畔信步走著。池塘中綻放著的蓮花，宛若玉石一般晶瑩可愛，一種無以形容的芳香，從花蕊裏不絕的向外飄漾著。此刻的極樂世界正是清晨。

不一會，釋迦佇立在池畔，從覆蓋於水面的蓮葉隙間，無意中看到池底下的情景。這極樂世界的蓮池下面，正是地獄的底層，因而透過水晶般瑩澈的水，宛如透過透視鏡一般，可以清楚的看到奈河和針山的情形。

THE SPIDER'S SILK

ONE DAY WHILE ŚĀKYAMUNI WAS SITTING IN A GARDEN BY THE SIDE OF A WELL, HIS EYES WERE DRAWN DEEP INTO THE WELL....

!

AHHHHHHH!

AHHHHHHH!

HELP! HELP ME! I'M SUFFERING TERRIBLY! OHH!...

THIS MAN MUST HAVE BEEN VERY EVIL DURING HIS LIFETIME TO SUFFER LIKE THIS IN HELL....

這時，地獄底層，一個叫犍陀多的漢子和別的罪人一起蠢動的模樣，落進釋迦的佛眼裏。這個叫犍陀多的漢子，過去雖是個殺人放火幹盡壞事的大盜，却也做過一件——唯一的一件善事。事情是這樣的，有一次，當他穿過森林的時候，發現一隻小蜘蛛在路旁爬行，犍陀多隨即抬起脚來，想踩死牠，却又突然改變了主意，他想：「不行，不行，蜘蛛雖小，也是有生命的。要是濫殺了它，也是怪可憐的。」而終於饒了蜘蛛的命。

釋迦牟尼一面瀏覽地獄的情景，一面記起犍陀多曾經放過蜘蛛的事。他想儘可能的把這漢子救出地獄，以酬報他的善行。釋迦往旁邊一望，正好發現翡翠色的蓮葉上，懸垂著一根極樂世界的蜘蛛吐出的美麗的銀絲。他便輕輕拈起那根蜘蛛絲，從玉一般晶瑩的白蓮隙間，筆直的垂入深邃的地獄底層。

這兒是地獄底層的血池，犍陀多跟其他的罪人在那兒乍浮乍沉著。到處都是闇黑一片，偶而朦朧隱現的亮光，也是令人不寒而慄的針山上閃爍的針光。那種恐怖是無以言宣的。加之，周遭宛似墳地那般死寂，

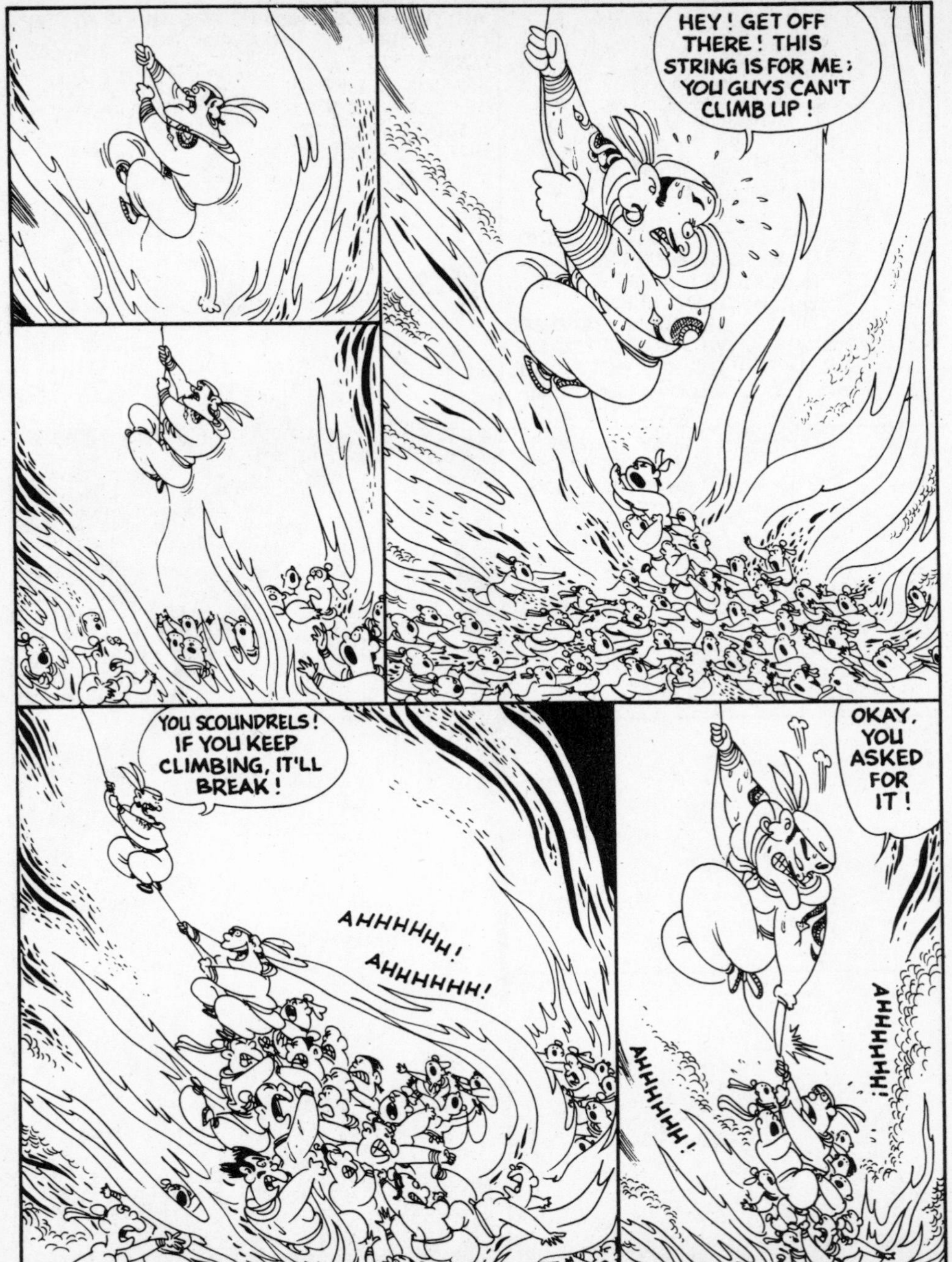

偶而聽到的，也只是罪人吐出的懨弱的嘆息。沉淪在這兒的罪人，都已遭到地獄的種種折磨而疲累不堪，連哭出聲的氣力都喪盡了。即使是大盜犍陀多，也在血池裏硬咽著，猶如瀕死的青蛙一味地扭動著身體。……………。（節自芥川龍之介「蜘蛛之絲」）

一天薄暮，一個傭工正站在羅生門下躲雨。

寬敞的城門下，除他沒有第二個人了。僅有一隻蟋蟀，停在處處紅漆斑剝了的大圓柱上。羅生門既在朱雀大路上，照理該有幾個戴高頂女笠或軟頭巾的人在那裡躲雨的，而竟除了他沒有第二個人。

這是近年來，京都因了地震、旋風、大火、饑饉等天災人禍接踵而來，使京中寥落得廻異尋常。據舊誌上的記載：佛像或供具被敲碎了，那些油漆或貼金的木頭，堆積在路邊，被當作柴薪來出售。京中的情況如此，羅生門的修繕被擱在一邊，當然誰也懶得去管了。而看中了這個荒涼，狐狸來此藏身，盜

賊來此棲止，到後來甚至沒有人認的死屍，也送到這個城樓上來拋棄了。因而到了日色西沈，即令人毛骨悚然，誰也不敢到這城門附近來走動了。

倒是不知道從那裡飛來的，許多烏鴉都齊集到這裡來。白天，不知道有多少，在空中畫着圓圈，繞着高蹺着的鴟尾，邊叫着在飛翔。當羅生門的上空被晚霞染上一片紅色時，牠們像是撒着芝麻一般，尤為清晰。烏鴉，當然是啄城樓上的死人肉來的。——但今天，也許是時刻已晚，一隻也看不到了。只是處處快要塌倒的，那些裂縫裡長着青草的石階上，這裡那裡留下來鴉糞的許多白點。傭工在共有九級石階的最上一級，把洗褪了顏色的藍夾襖墊在屁股下，一面關心着右頰上那顆偌大青春痘，茫然望着兩脚。

剛才作者雖説「傭工在躲雨」，但雨便停了，他也沒有什麼特別的去處。平時，該是回主人家的時候，但四、五天前，他被那個主人解雇了。上面曾説過的，當時京都市面的衰微無以復加。現在這個傭工之被多年雇用的主人解雇，事實上只是這個衰微的小小餘波罷了。所以與其説：「傭工在躲雨」，倒不如説「被雨趕着的傭工，前途茫茫無處可去」來得恰當。再加上，今天的天色，對於這個平安朝的傭工底 Sentimentalisme，也影響非淺。從中刻開始落的雨，迄無停止的模樣。於是，傭工比什麼都迫切

I-I WAS.... JUST COLLECTING SOME HAIR.
THE POOR GIRL'S DEAD, ISN'T IT BAD ENOUGH ALREADY WITHOUT YOU DEFILING HER CORPSE?
BUT THE HAIR CAN BE SOLD FOR MONEY THAT I CAN USE TO BUY FOOD....
MAYBE IT'S A TERRIBLE THING TO PULL HAIR FROM A CORPSE, BUT THESE DEAD PEOPLE WEREN'T ALL THAT GOOD WHEN THEY WERE ALIVE ANYWAY. LIKE HER--SHE USED TO DRY SNAKE MEAT AND SELL IT AS EEL....
BUT I DON'T THINK WHAT SHE DID WAS ALL THAT BAD, BECAUSE IF SHE HADN'T DONE IT, SHE WOULD HAVE STARVED TO DEATH. SHE HAD NO CHOICE!
AND I'M JUST LIKE HER, IF I DON'T DO IT, I'LL STARVE. WHAT CHOICE DO I HAVE?... PLEASE FORGIVE ME!

的，便是明天的生活如何打發……。

要使一籌莫展的事打開僵局，不讓你有選擇手段的餘裕。倘或選擇，唯有餓死在泥牆脚下或路邊的泥塗中。之後，被送到這個城樓上，像狗一般地拋棄罷了。倘或不擇手段——傭工的想法，在同一條路上不知低徊了多少次，好不容易才到達了這個僻角。但這「倘或」，永遠地，結局還是「倘或」。傭工雖是肯定了不擇手段，為了給這「倘或」下個論斷，跟着而來的必然的結果便是「除非做賊」，但他却鼓不起勇氣來作積極的肯定。……。（節自芥川龍之介小說「羅生門」）

Guide to Pronunciation

There are different systems of romanization of Chinese words, but in all of these systems the sounds of letters used do not necessarily correspond to those sounds that we are accustomed to using in English (for instance, would you have guessed that *zh* is pronounced like *j*?). Of course, these systems can be learned, but to save some time and effort for the reader who is not a student of Chinese, we have provided the following pronunciation guide.

The Chinese words appear on the left as they do in the text and are followed by their pronunciations. Just sound out the pronunciations as you would for an unfamiliar English word, and you will be quite close to the proper Mandarin pronunciation.

Japanese and Sanskrit words also appear in the list below and are identified as such. However, since their romanizations are much closer to our English pronunciations, a guide is not provided. As for the diacritical marks, an accent (´) above an s in Sanskrit indicates an *sh* sound and a macron (¯) above a vowel indicates a drawn out vowel sound in both Japanese and Sanskrit.

Notes:

-*dz* is a combination of a *d* and a *z* in one sound, without the *ee* sound at the end; so it sounds kind of like a bee in flight with a slight *d* sound at the beginning.
-*ts* is also a combination, which is mostly the *ss* sound, with a slight *t* sound at the beginning.
-*ew* is pronounced like the *ew* in f*ew*.
-*ow* is pronounced like the *ow* in n*ow*.

Amitābha (Sanskrit)
Ānanda (Sanskrit)
Anhui: on-hway
Arhat (Sanskrit)

Bai Juyi: buy jew (*ew* as in f*ew*)-ee
Baiyun: buy-ewn (*ew* as in f*ew*)
Baizhang: buy-jong
Baling: bah (*a* as in f*a*ther)-leeng
Bankei (Japanese)
Bo Ya: bwo (*o* as in m*o*re) yah (*a* as in f*a*ther)
Bodhidharma (Sanskrit)
Bodhisattva (Sanskrit)
Buddha (Sanskrit)
Buddha-dharma (Sanskrit)

Cao: tsow (rhymes with *now*)
Caoxi: tsow (rhymes with *now*)-shee
Chaling Yu: chah (*a* as in f*a*ther)-leeng ew (as in f*ew*)
Chan: chon
Chih Chung: jir jong (long o)
Cishou: ts-sho (long o)
Congshen: tsong (long o)-shun
Cuiwei: tsway-way

Dahui Zonggao: dah (*a* as in f*a*ther)-hway dzong (long o)-gow (as in g*ow*n)
Daigan (Japanese)
Damei: dah (*a* as in f*a*ther)-may
Danxia: don-shyaw
Dao: dow
Daowu: dow-oo
Dapo: dah (*a* as in f*a*ther)-pwo (*o* as in m*o*re)
Dharma (Sanskrit)
Dokuon (Japanese)

Deshan: du (*u* as in p*u*ll)-shawn
Dongshan: dong (long o)-shawn

Eshun (Japanese)

Fayun: fah (*a* as in f*a*ther)-ewn (*ew* as in f*ew*)

Guanyin: gwon-een
Gautama (Sanskrit)

Hakuin (Japanese)
Hebei: hu (*u* as in p*u*ll)-bay
Hongen: hong (long o)-un
Huangbo: hwong-bwo (*o* as in m*o*re)
Huinęng: hway-nung
Huilin: hway-leen
Hunan: hoo-non

Ikkyū (Japanese)

Jianyuan: jyen-ywen
Jiannan: jyen-non
Jingqing: jeeng-cheeng
Jingshan: jeeng-shon
Juzhi: jew (*ew* as in f*ew*)-jir

Kāśyapa (Sanskrit)
Kitagaki (Japanese)
Kyōto (Japanese)

Li Ao: lee ow (as in n*ow*)
Li Bo: lee bwo (*o* as in m*o*re)
Liangjie: lyong-jyeh
Linji: leen-jee
Longtan: long (long o)-ton (as in *ton*sil)

Mokusen (Japanese)

Nanin (Japanese)
Nanquan: non-chwen
Niaowo: nyow (rhymes with *now*)-wo (*o* as in m*o*re)
Nirvāṇa (Sanskrit)

Pang: pong
Panshan: pon-shon

Qianfeng: chyen-fung
Qinglong: cheeng-long (long o)
Qingping: cheeng-peeng
Qingzhou: cheeng-joe

Rashōmon (Japanese)
Ryōkan (Japanese)

Śākyamuni (Sanskrit)
Samādhi (Sanskrit)
Śārira (Sanskrit)
Sengai (Japanese)
Shandong: shon-dong (long o)
Shanneng: shon-nung
Shichiri (Japanese)
Shigong: sure-gong (long o)
Shiji: sure-jee
Shishuang: sure-shwong
Shitou Xiquan: sure-toe shee-chwen
Shiyan: sure-yen
Shōkoku (Japanese)
Shouchu: sho (long o)-choo
Sichuan: sz-chwon
Siddhārtha Gautama (Sanskrit)
Song: song (long o)
Sumeru (Sanskrit)
Sūtra (Sanskrit)

Tang: tong
Tsai: tsigh (rhymes with *high*)

Vimalakīrti-Nirdeśa (Sanskrit)

Wei: way
Weiyan: way-yen
Wuji: oo-jee
Wujincang: oo-jeen-tsong

Xiangyan Zhixian: shyong-yen jir-shyen
Xing: sheeng
Xitang: shee-tong
Xuansha: shwen-shah
Xuanjian: shwen-jyen
Xuanze: shwen-zu (*u* as in p*u*ll)

Yang Fu: yong foo
Yangqi: yong-chee
Yangshan: yong-shon
Yangtze: yong-ts
Yaoshan: yow (rhymes with *now*)-shon
Yishan: ee-shon
Yixuan: ee-shwen
YiZhong: ee-jong (long o)
Yunyan: ewn (*ew* as in f*ew*)-yen
Yunyou: ewn (*ew* as in f*ew*)-yo
Yutang: ew (*ew* as in f*ew*)-tong

Zen (Japanese)
Zhang Zhuo: jong jwo (*o* as in more
Zhaozhou: jow (as in *jow*l)-joe
Zhenzhou: jun-joe
Zhicang: jir-tsong
Zhimen: jir-mun
Zhishang: jir-shong
Zhong Ziqi: jong (long o) dz-chee
Zhou: joe
Zhuangzi: jwong-dz